Honoring the men and women of the allied armed forces and their families who have for centuries protected the United States, Britain, and France.

LEST WE FORGET

MASTERPIECES OF

PATRIOTIC JEWELRY

AND MILITARY DECORATIONS

Judith Price

President of the National Jewelry Institute

TAYLOR TRADE PUBLISHING
LANHAM · NEW YORK · BOULDER · TORONTO · PLYMOUTH, UK

Published by Taylor Trade Publishing
An imprint of The Rowman & Littlefield Publishing Group, Inc.
4501 Forbes Boulevard, Suite 200, Lanham, Maryland 20706
http://www.rlpgtrade.com

Estover Road, Plymouth PL6 7PY, United Kingdom

Distributed by National Book Network

Copyright © 2011 by Judith Price
Interior design by Corinda Cook
Typography: Requiem, Univers, and Goudy

British Library Cataloguing in Publication Information Available

Library of Congress Cataloging-in-Publication Data Is Available
ISBN 978-1-58979-686-7 (cloth : alk. paper)

∞™ The paper used in this publication meets the minimum requirements of American National Standard for Information Sciences—Permanence of Paper for Printed Library Materials, ANSI/NISO Z39.48-1992.

Printed in China

(Page 1)
Diamond Eagle Pin
Maker unknown
United States, c. 1812–1820
Gold, silver, diamonds
W: 9.5 cm
Courtesy of A La Vieille Russie

(Table of Contents, page 5)
Insignia of the Order of the Iron Crown
    of Napoléon I
François-Regnault Nitot
France, c. 1810
Diamonds, enamel, gold, rubies, sapphires
L: 5.5 cm; W: 3.3 cm
Musée de l'Armée

CONTENTS

INTRODUCTION

Five years ago the National Jewelry Institute staged the exhibition *Treasures of the Titans*, made unique by its display of personal objects belonging to renowned and often controversial figures such as Winston Churchill, Lawrence of Arabia, and George S. Patton. For the show we managed to borrow Patton's 1916 ivory-handled "Peacemaker" Colt .45 pistol from the Patton Museum of Cavalry and Armor in Fort Knox pictured on page 7—a major coup, considering the museum had never before permitted its removal. Sharing a devotion to country and honor, the owners of these pieces were *sui generis* and larger than life, often rattling more than a few cages on their paths to glory. As we celebrated *Treasures of the Titans* over dinner, George Patton Waters, the famous general's grandson, said that his grandfather and I would have seen something of ourselves in each other. Being familiar with histories of the man and the soldier, I could not help swelling with pride, thinking of his oft-quoted motto for the men in his Third Army: "*L'audace,*

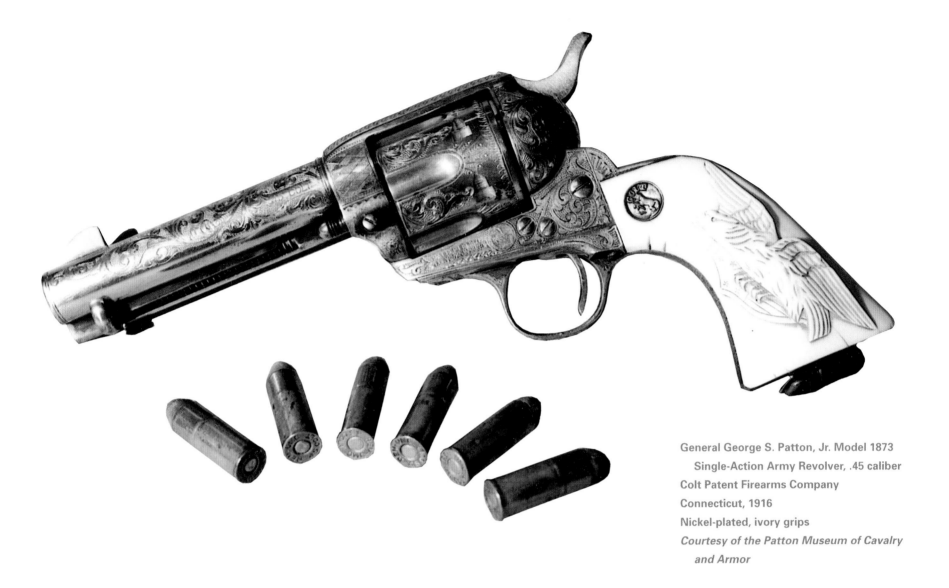

General George S. Patton, Jr. Model 1873
Single-Action Army Revolver, .45 caliber
Colt Patent Firearms Company
Connecticut, 1916
Nickel-plated, ivory grips
*Courtesy of the Patton Museum of Cavalry
and Armor*

l'audace, toujours audace" ("Audacity, audacity, always audacity"). Spirit and drive were also the marching orders for my staff when I founded and managed an international magazine group for 25 years. The Patton experience inspired me to further explore to the stories of American patriots, and those of our allies, and to give a glimpse of their triumphs and struggles and defeats, through the pieces of jewelry that came to make up a collection of which I am most proud: *Lest We Forget: Masterpieces of Patriotic Jewelry and Military Decorations*.

For ages, jewelry has commemorated significant moments of war and peace, dating back to the ancient Near East, when wreaths adorned sculptures to symbolize rank and power. A shining example is the headdress of Queen Pu-Abi (page 8), prominently featuring her gold laurel symbol of royal authority, dating back to the cradle of civilization at the Mesopotamian city of Ur, from 2650 B.C. The laurel, derived from the Latin *laus* for praise, remains a symbol of civilian achievement or military distinction, like the U.S. Medal of Honor, which consists of a gold star surrounded by a wreath. The very word "baccalaureate" traces its origins to military roots from the Latin *baccalaureus* (young man aspiring to knighthood). Ironically symbolizing both war and peace, the laurel adorns the emblems of both the United Nations and the Nobel Peace Prize and yet is also a hallmark of the American Military Order of Foreign Wars.

Lest We Forget: Masterpieces of Patriotic Jewelry and Military Decorations chronicles war, valor, memories, and peace with the decorations, objects, and jewelry that recall the triumph and terrors that defined our borders, our century, and those preceding it. Through cannon fire and rifle smoke, above the battle cries and the bugle's tune, we return to the wars that shaped America and the small treasures that mark them. We owe the preservation of these archives to prominent lending institutions and organizations from the United States, Britain, and France including: the American Folk Art Museum, the American Numismatic Society, the British Museum, the Dwight D. Eisenhower Presidential Library & Museum, the Imperial War Museum, the Musée

de l'Armée, the National Army Museum, the Natural History Museum of Los Angeles County, the Patton Museum of Cavalry and Armor, the Victoria and Albert Museum, and the West Point Museum; the patrimony of such leading firms as A La Vieille Russie, Alfred Dunhill, Boucheron, Cartier, Chaumet, Hermès, Historical Design, Oscar Heyman, Tiffany & Co.; The Ledoux Napoléon Collection; and private lenders.

The text of *Lest We Forget: Masterpieces of Patriotic Jewelry and Military Decorations* is supplemented by interviews with experts from these institutions, including: Philip Attwood, Keeper of Coins and Medals, the British Museum; Lieutenant-Colonel Christophe Bertrand, Conservateur, World Wars Department, Musée de l'Armée; Robert Wilson Hoge, Curator of North American Coins and Currency, American Numismatic Society; collector Bruno Ledoux; Yvonne Markowitz, Rita J. and Susan B. Kaplan Curator of Jewelry, Museum of Fine Arts in Boston; Michael McAfee, Curator of History, West Point Museum; and Fergus Read,

Headdress of Queen Pu-Abi
Maker unknown
Ur, 2650–2550 B.C.E.
Gold, lapis lazuli, carnelian (displayed on a
    mannequin)
The University of Pennsylvania Museum
    Image 152100

Head of the Department of Collections Access, Imperial War Museum. These insights will expand upon the role jewelry and decorations have played in commemorating the history of war and peace.

World renowned institutions such as the British Museum and the Victoria and Albert in London are flooded with visitors, but more specialized military museums often go unappreciated. This book would not be possible without the generosity of many such museums.

Only one hour by car from New York City is the West Point Museum. It boasts the "oldest and largest diversified public collection of militaria in the Western Hemisphere," with collections predating the founding of the U.S. Military Academy at West Point, including captured artillery from the British defeat at Saratoga in 1777. The

Society of Cincinnati Medal
Presented to Henry Dearborn
Maker unknown
Origin Unknown, c. 1870
Gold, enamel, silk ribbon
Pendant: W: 2.9 cm; H: 4.4 cm; Ribbon: W: 3.8 cm
West Point Museum Collection, United States Military Academy, West Point, New York

collection ranges from such unique and famous pieces as Washington's pistols and the ivory and diamond Field Marshal's baton of Hermann Göring to the fatigue uniform and equipment of the ordinary Vietnam War "grunt."

The American Numismatic Society maintains a small gallery, a library, and its cabinet at 75 Varick Street in New York City, as well as a major exhibition on the history of money at the Federal Reserve Bank of New York at 33 Liberty Street. Founded more than 150 years ago, the collection houses approximately 800,000 coins, medals and other objects, and a library of 100,000 numismatic books. It is open to the public for consultation by making an appointment with the librarian or a curator. The collection and library catalogues are available online at www.numismatics.org.

The National Jewelry Institute is planning an exhibition onboard The Intrepid Sea, Air & Space Museum, which is located at 12th Avenue and 46th Street in New York City. Commissioned in 1943, the aircraft carrier USS *Intrepid* and her crew served in World War II, the Space Race, the Cold War, and the Vietnam War. The newly renovated museum complex also includes the USS *Growler* submarine and British Airways Concorde. A vast collection of thirty restored Navy, Marine Corps, Army, Coast Guard, and international aircraft are visible throughout the Museum. In 2011 the *Intrepid* was chosen as the new home for *Enterprise* (OV-101), the first Space Shuttle Orbiter. Spanning the length of four city blocks, Intrepid features spectacular interactive exhibits and innovative virtual, multisensory, and video technology for an experience that thrills as it educates, moves you through history as it moves your heart, inspires as it entertains.

The Hôtel National des Invalides complex in Paris is an extraordinary museum. Built by Louis XIV in 1670, and originally housing more than 6,000 of the Sun King's aged or injured soldiers, it is now a central tourist destination, viewed for its astounding architecture, tombs—Napoléon is buried here, as well as most of France's military heroes, including the composer of "La Marseillaise"—and historical significance (it continues its tradition as a hospital, with a small section dedicated as a center for handicapped or disabled war veterans). Significantly, the Hôtel houses the Musée de l'Armée, the only location where citizens of France could publicly view their flag during the German occupation. Exhibits range from antique military treasures to uniforms and paintings from the First and Second World Wars. The museum displays an exceptional range of swords, crossbows, and pistols from medieval times to Napoléon's reign. In 2008 the Musée de l'Armée opened the Historial Charles de Gaulle, an audiovisual gallery that retraces de Gaulle's journey through the twentieth century.

The focus of the Imperial War Museum is British and Commonwealth campaigns since 1914, with an emphasis on the World Wars. The museum first opened in London in 1920, and now there are further sites near Manchester and Cambridge, as well as HMS *Belfast* and the Churchill Museum, also in London. The collection consists of more than 19,000 fine art pieces; 15,000 diaries, letters, and memoirs; more than 10 million photographs; as well as object collections including uniforms, tanks, aircraft, artillery, and hundreds of orders, decorations, and medals. The Museum has nearly 250 Victoria Crosses. Most are from the collection of Lord John Ashcroft. The Museum also contains a collection of heavy military equipment, artillery, ammunition, uniforms, and firearms. A Holocaust section, added to the main London site in 1999, documents Nazi atrocities and highlights the survivors of their persecution.

The National Army Museum was established by Royal Charter in 1960 to collect, preserve, and exhibit objects and records relating to the Regular and Auxiliary forces of the British Army and of the Commonwealth, and to encourage research into their history and traditions. Originally housed at the Royal Military Academy Sandhurst, the first phase of a purpose-built museum opened in 1971 on a site near Sloane Square leased from the Commissioners of the Royal Hospital Chelsea. A second phase was completed in 1980. The galleries explore the history of Britain and its army from the medieval period to the present day in a series of chronological displays. There is also a separate art gallery showing the Museum's larger and more important canvases. Further details and a summary account of the collections may be found on the Museum website (www.nam.ac.uk).

The National Jewelry Institute has conducted seventeen exhibitions. Our most prominent exhibitions are commemorated in the *Masterpieces* series of books. The first, *Masterpieces of American Jewelry*, opened in New York and then traveled to major museums in London, Paris, and Pittsburgh. *Masterpieces of French Jewelry* followed in New York and then went on to San Francisco. *Masterpieces of Ancient Jewelry: Exquisite Objects from the Cradle of Civilization* launched in New York and then traveled to Chicago.

WAR

While military service was a valued tradition throughout the European aristocracy, the United States' break with Europe's values and the notion of an aristocracy has made George S. Patton's military ancestry a rare example in the course of American history. His great-great grandfather, Robert Patton, immigrated to the States from Scotland in the 1760s but declined to serve in the Continental Army. His son John Mercer Patton, an attorney, fathered nine children, eight of whom would fight in Virginia for the Confederacy against the North. One of them was Colonel George Patton who, according to author Robert Patton in his family history of the Pattons, was called by his men "one brave and noble commander . . . as courteous a gentleman as God ever created." Attending military colleges like West Point and Annapolis, this generation provided the foundation for the family military history, leading to the birth in 1885 of the third George S. Patton the first to attend the Virginia Military Institute. The future commander of the famous 3RD army in WWII was known to his family as "the boy" or "Georgie."

In 1904, when George Patton was a West Point cadet, he ironically characterized the brutality and romance of war in a letter to his father: "I am very much disheartened by the wonderful efficiency of the modern rifle . . . as there is now talk of them making a gun which fires 20 shots a second. I don't exactly see how war is to be carried on against such obstacles . . . but when I am a great general I would bury the man who invented rapid fire guns and by doing so ruined the beauty of war."

There are numerous pieces of jewelry and decorations in this collection recording moments in that history, from revolutionary to contemporary, including both the romantic as well as the brutal. One of the earliest pieces depicting wartime in the United States is a British medal dedicating the Old Middle Dutch Church in New York as a riding school by the British Colony (1776–1783) on page 13. Their congregation supported the Revolution, encouraging ministers to speak out for the colonists. However, after the first major battle of the Revolution, the

Commemorative Medal
Maker unknown
Origin unknown, 1776–1783
Gilt metal
D: 3.4 cm
*On loan courtesy of the Council of
  the National Army Museum, London*

Battle of Long Island, known also as the Battle of Brooklyn, these activists fled Manhattan. This battle, the first engagement between the American and British forces, was in fact the largest conflict of the war. More than 32,000 men from the British Army forced Washington's retreat from Brooklyn to Manhattan, which led to the withdrawal of his entire army to New Jersey and Pennsylvania. When the British occupied Manhattan in 1776, they used the Middle Church as a prison, later converting it to the riding academy where British officials could improve their combat skills.

During the same revolutionary period, colonists in New York started an anti-British organization: The Society of Tammany, named for Tamanend, a Native American leader of the Lenape. According to historian Edwin Kilroe, author of *Saint Tammany and the Origin of the Society of Tammany*: "Under the favoring leadership of Thomas Jefferson and James Madison the movement flourished, and its organized activities foreshadowed the establishment of national political machines." A chapter was formed in each of the thirteen states as a secret, patriotic brotherhood also known as the Columbian Order. The original Columbian Order commemorating Columbus was preempted by the more popular identity derived from the name of the American Indian chief to underscore its patriotic origins. After the Revolution, the Society, organized by William Mooney, became a fraternal organization, often called Tammany Hall, after the name of their building located on East 14TH Street, between 3RD Avenue and Irving Place. Their leadership delved in politics, courting immigrants to gain votes. The Columbian Order Medal of the Society of the Tammany on pages 14 and 15, is extremely rare. On the front are a coiled rattlesnake and the words: "COLUMBIAN ORDER INSTITUTED." The word "BEWARE" is written on a ribbon in the center with the date, 1789, on the bottom. On the back appear the words: "WHERE LIBERTY DWELLS THERE IS MY COUNTRY/OCT. 12. A.D. 1492." On the left is a Native American wearing a feathered headdress and around him is

Columbian Order (Tammany) Badge (back)
John Pearson
United States, 1789
Silver
D: 4.2 cm
Courtesy of The American Numismatic Society

Napoléonic Regimental Eagle
Maker unknown
France, 1804
Cast bronze
H: 22 cm; W: 25 cm; L: 14 cm
Private Collection

It was Napoléon's policy to personally present all of the eagles for display. Three models were presented during the first empire. This is an example of the first model from 1804. Today 124 examples of the 1804 pattern eagle are known to exist—forty-six in French museums, ten in British museums, fifty-five in worldwide museums and thirteen in private collections.

a garment of animal tails or feathers. He smokes a peace pipe and offers his left hand to a European, who wears seventeenth-century garments, carries a sword, and holds a flagstaff in his hand.

During the same period in Europe, craftsmen began to produce military objects for Napoléon Bonaparte. Napoléon, who was born in Corsica, trained at the École Militaire in Paris. In his first military operation as an artillery captain, he forced British naval ships to retreat. In a Northern Italian campaign in 1796, he teamed up with French Marshal André Masséna, Duc de Rivoli, in the famous Battle of Rivoli. In Arcola, General Bonaparte personally led the assault across the Arcola Bridge, inspiring his troops on to victory with his bravery. The famous three-day battle of the French against the Austrian armies is often commemorated with the image of Napoléon bearing a flag as he leads the charge over Arcola Bridge. Thereafter he installed himself as First Consul; with clever political maneuvering and by publishing two newspapers, Napoléon finally had the power to crown himself Emperor in 1804.

Napoléon wanted an emblem for his new regime. On page 16 is a bronze and gilded eagle with open wings and a thunderbolt under its right talon. While there were debates whether the new emblem should be an eagle, a lion, or an elephant, Napoléon chose the eagle as it was the symbol of Ancient Rome and was associated with military victory. After Napoléon was crowned, he imposed an eagle standard on top of every flag. Demonstrating the importance Napoléon attached to powerful rich symbols is the pair of epaulettes of a sapper captain on page 19. Made of gold bullion, this is the only surviving example of its kind.

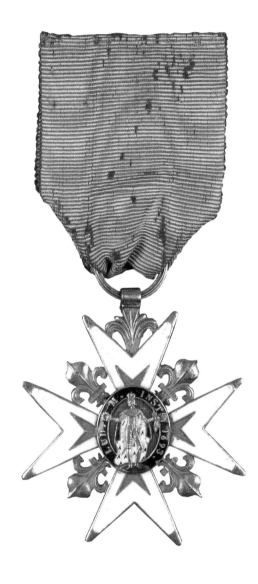

Lafayette's Cross from the Order of Saint-Louis
Maker unknown
France, eighteenth century
Gold, enamel, textile
L: 8.5 cm; W: 4.0 cm
Musée de l'Armée

Lieutenant-Colonel Christophe Bertrand

Lieutenant-Colonel Christophe Bertrand is the curator of the Département des Deux Guerres Mondiales (Department of the Two World Wars) at the Musée de l'Armée in Paris. He joined the department after a career in the General Army as a staff officer.

One of the objects from your department is the Insignia of the Order of the Iron Crown of Napoléon I (page 5). What distinguished the decorations and designs of this period from those of the next century?

The orders of the Empire were conferred exclusively according to one's merits. It differed with those granted under the Ancien Régime, which were in some cases given only under certain conditions of lineage.

For that matter, when in 1802 Napoléon Bonaparte created the Légion d'honneur, the Jacobins reacted violently. They saw it as a coming back to the values of the Ancien Régime. For him, this distinction rewards above all the services rendered by civilians and militaries.

Another object is Lafayette's Order of Saint-Louis (page 17). Lafayette was an officer in George Washington's army. What motivated his alliance with the U.S. Revolution?

France joined the War of Independence with the American forces fundamentally to take revenge on Great Britain.

Previously, France signed the Treaty of Paris with Great Britain in 1763 that ended the French and Indian War/Seven Years War. As a consequence of this Treaty, France lost almost all its territories in America (Canada, the Great Lakes, area west of the Mississippi).

Another object is a U.S. medal honoring Maréchal Philippe Pétain for his service in the Great War (page 20). What was his contribution to French military history so Americans can better understand it?

Maréchal Pétain was an integral part in French military history for two reasons.

First, he was one of the victors of the Battle of Verdun, along with General Nivelle and General de Castelnau. The victory, after more than eleven months of fierce and bloody battles, brought a stop to a German offensive whose aim was "to bleed dry the French army."

But above all, Maréchal Pétain played an important role during the great mutinies of 1917 that struck the French army after the bloody offensives of "Le Chemin des Dames."

(continued on page 20)

18

Pair of Sapper Captain's Epaulettes
Maker unknown
France, 1804
Gold bullion including fringe
L: 13 cm; W: 11 cm
Private Collection

This medal was presented to Maréchal Pétain in 1931 to commemorate the 150th anniversary of the Battle of Yorktown.

150th Anniversary of Yorktown
Campaign Medal of Maréchal Pétain
Maker unknown
United States, 1931
Metal, textile
L: 11.5 cm; W: 5.2 cm
Musée de l'Armée

From the time of Pétain's appointment as head of the French armies, he acted firmly to reduce the number of soldiers executed for mutiny. He made an important series of decisions in order to improve the day to day life of the soldiers, exhausted by more than three years of war, and he stopped the strategically inefficient and life-wasting offensives.

Pétain was awarded the title of Maréchal of France on November 19, 1918. The popularity he enjoyed at that moment, among the soldiers and ex-servicemen, cannot be questioned.

Another object from that period is a baton of Maréchal Ferdinand Foch. What is the significance of a baton and is it still used today?

The République just like the Ancien Régime, and the First and Second Empire established the military dignity of Maréchal.

This supreme rank is granted on a President's proposal, after having been unanimously voted by the Assemblée Nationale, to the Généraux, who commanded victoriously an army to the battlefront.

Three Généraux were granted the dignity of Maréchal of France during the Great War: Général Joffre, Général Foch, and Général Pétain. Général Foch, Commander-in-Chief of the Allied Army

Forces, was promoted Maréchal of France on August 23, 1918. At the end of the war, he benefited from high international recognition. On July 19, 1919, he received the military title of Field Marshal (Marshal of the United Kingdom) and was granted the title of Marshal of Poland in April 1923. In the U.S., the Knights of Columbus, a Catholic Charity Society, granted him the title of Honorary Member, and in 1919 awarded him a Baton of Honour from Tiffany inspired by the french model. The dignity of Maréchal is symbolized by the presentation of the baton on page 71 of royal blue enamel, decorated with 30 gold stars. Its heads are rings of gold, inscribed at one end with: *Terror Belli, Decus Pacis* ("Terror of the War, Honor of the Peace"), and on the other with the Maréchal's name and the date of his appointment.

Général Charles de Gaulle is widely known to Americans. What distinguished his career from the great French military officers who preceded him?

After graduating from l'Ecole Spéciale Militaire of Saint Cyr in 1912, Général de Gaulle enjoyed a career similar to other officers of his generation who intended to be in high positions within the Army.

De Gaulle was Company Commander during the Great War, Chief of the 19th "Chasseurs à pied" battalion at military school in 1922, various posts as Staff Officer in France and Syria, Colonel in 1937 of the 507th tank battalion, and Commander of the 4th reserve battleship division during the May-June 1940 campaign of France. Named Temporary Brigadier Général on June 1, 1940, he acted as the Under-secretary of State of War and National Defense under Paul Reynaud.

When Maréchal Pétain's government decided to sign the Armistice, de Gaulle went to London and, on June 18th, he asked all his compatriots to continue the fight against the occupying forces. From this moment, the soldier became a politician. Général de Gaulle was no longer a regular general officer under the authority of the legal government and bound to the reserve's duty. He broke with the Vichy government and the military institution. After having gathered, organized and managed the Free French Army with the Allied Forces during World War II, de Gaulle embarked on a campaign to direct the French Provisional Government between 1944 and 1946, and then take on the role of Président de la République from 1958 to 1969.

Napoléon as man and general is the subject of an interview with French collector Bruno Ledoux on page 62. The Artistic Director of the Manufacture d'Armes de Versaille, Nicolas-Noël Boutet (1761–1833) created the pistols on page 22. Celebrated for their intricate workmanship and technical perfection, the pistols were made in 1805 in the Versailles Imperial Arms Factory and are composed of wood, steel, gold, and silver. Napoléon appointed Major Général Martin Vignolle Minister of War of the Cisalpine Republic, a French puppet state in Northern Italy, which remained an independent republic until 1802. As Minister, Vignolle received the most magnificent sword mount (page 23), composed of gilded metal, enamel, and diamonds. The Republic known as Cisalpine Gaul is today the most northern area of Italy, encompassing

Sword Mount and Sheath Ornaments of Vignolle
Awarded by the Cisalpine Republic
Italy, 1797
Gilded metal, enamel, diamonds
Musée de l'Armée

23

major provinces like Lombardy, Piedmont, and Liguria. Cisalpine Gaul, literally "Gaul on this side of the Alps," was therefore a major responsibility for which its Minister was recognized and rewarded as a grand officer of the Légion d'honneur and made a Count of the Empire.

In June of 1812 the United States, barely in its thirties, declared war on Britain. There were many causes: restrictions imposed by Britain on U.S. trade with France; forced British recruitment of U.S. citizens into the Royal Navy; and British military support of natives who were resisting the expansion of the American frontier into the Northwest. The U.S. was not prepared for a war it was obliged to fight in a variety of theatres—along the Atlantic coast, on the frontier, along the Gulf of Mexico, and in its newly independent cities. Possibly attributed to an ex-patriot English jeweler working in the U.S. at the time of the war, the diamond eagle pin on page 24 projects the tension of the confrontation. The American

Diamond Eagle Pin
Maker unknown
United States, c. 1812–1820
Gold, silver, diamonds
W: 9.5 cm
Courtesy of A La Vieille Russie

eagle clasps arrows in both claws instead of an olive branch, which would traditionally occupy the right talon.

In the summer of 1814, during the War of 1812, the British advanced on Washington D.C. burning down the White House and the Treasury, and proceeded to attack Baltimore from September 7TH to 14TH. A portrayal of this battle is recorded in the glorious watercolor on ivory pin on page 26. Just before dawn on September 14TH after a heavy rain, the British gave up the assault, when Baltimore's Fort McHenry refused to surrender. Georgetown lawyer, Francis Scott Key, whose father was a judge and an officer in the Continental Army, was inspired by the sight of the U.S. flag flying over the fort to write a poem that became America's National Anthem. On his sloop, returning to Baltimore from the British ship HMS *Tonnant,* where he'd negotiated a prisoner exchange, Key witnessed unwavering American forces at Fort McHenry as they were bombarded by Britain's artillery inspiring the song's signature "bombs bursting in air."

The mission of the General Society of the War of 1812 was to "perpetuate the memory and spirit" of the veterans of the War of 1812. Membership was open to any person twenty-one years of age who served in the war or was a lineal descendant thereof.

General Society of the War of 1812 Medal
Maker unknown
Origin unknown, c. 1880
Gilt bronze, enamels, silk ribbon
Pendant: W: 3.2 cm; H: 3.8 cm / Ribbon: L: 7.6 cm
West Point Museum Collection, United
States Military, West Point, New York

Pin with Miniature of Soldiers
Artist unidentified
United States, Mid-nineteenth century
Watercolor on ivory
L: 3.2 cm; W: 2.5 cm
Collection, American Folk Art Museum, New York
Joseph Martinson Memorial Fund, Frances and Paul Martinson
   1981.12.29

While "The Star-Spangled Banner" is replete with bombs bursting and rockets' red glare, the French National Anthem, composed by Claude-Joseph Rouget de Lisle in 1792, became the rallying call of the French Revolution and is even more provocative. It was actually banned for decades by Napoléon I, Louis XVIII, and Napoléon III because the song is about the common man and not a royal subject. As one of the goriest and most passionate national anthems, the first stanza reads:

Arise children of the fatherland

The day of glory has arrived.

Against us tyranny's bloody banner is raised

Listen to the sound in the fields,

The howling of these fearsome soldiers.

They are coming into our midst

To cut the throats of your sons and wives.

Refrain:

To arms citizens

Form your battalions

Let us march, let us march

Let tainted blood water our fields.

Known as "The Marseillaise," the verses were first sung by soldiers marching from Marseille to Paris. By 1879, nine years after Napoléon III was deposed as Emperor and the Third Republic was established, it was restored as France's national anthem.

American-made jewelry and decorations did not begin to proliferate the United States until the Civil War. The first examples were, by European standards, base and primitive. The American style reflected its frontier origins. Without a professional military tradition or standing armies, most soldiers were farmers or laborers, as were jewelry craftsmen.

The Civil War, the bloodiest conflict in American history, saw the death of 360,000 soldiers on the Union side and 260,000 Confederates, with hundreds of thousands more injured. The number of those who perished during the Civil War nearly equals the total number of American soldiers killed in every other action up to the present. These thousands of citizen soldiers did not possess the uniforms of a European standing army, so each volunteer unit forged its unique identity by fashioning badges. Civil War Corps badges were originally made in cloth, later in bone or flattened bullets. Jewelers, like Tiffany, designed them to be affixed to hats. The badges served as identifiers, avoiding confusion among under-clothed armies.

Michael McAfee

Michael McAfee is the Curator of History at the West Point Museum. He is the Senior Advisory Editor of *Military Images* magazine and writes a continuing series entitled "Uniforms & History." He has overseen the museum's major exhibitions and catalogues.

One of the first American military decorations, the Cincinnati Medal (page 9), was accorded to officers of the Continental Army headquartered in the Hudson Highlands near West Point. Tell us about what action occurred immediately around West Point and why it was established as the institution we know today.

The insignia of the Society of the Cincinnati is not a military decoration. It is essentially an elaborate and beautiful medal showing membership in the Society which was organized as a fraternal order of American and French officers who served together in the American Revolution.

The stated purpose of the organization was to preserve and perpetuate the mutual friendships formed during the war. Because most of the American officers had come from the citizenry, they chose the symbolism of the ancient Roman hero Lucius Quintus Cincinnatus who left his plow and home to defend Rome from her enemies.

The Aztec Club medals, like the one shown on page 29 commemorate service in the War with Mexico. What was the origin of that conflict which these images recall?

The War with Mexico, which began in 1846, was precipitated by our "Manifest Destiny" of national expansion which led to a border dispute with Mexico after the Republic of Texas became a state. The admission of Texas was also a thorny issue in the United States as it added to the slave-owning states at a time when the Slavery Question was becoming more heated. While our military successes in that conflict generated another round of military fraternalism resulting in the creation of the Aztec Club, it can be argued that the war also set the stage for the coming Civil War.

The Order of the Dragon recalls American engagement in China. What was the U.S. role in the Boxer Rebellion? Who was designated to serve?

In 1900, in response to foreign political, social and economic interferences, Chinese nationalists who were improperly termed "Boxers" attacked Europeans, Japanese and Americans in China. The foreign embassies in Peking (now Beijing) were attacked and besieged. A multi-national force which included American soldiers and Marines

was sent to their relief. The Charlton Heston motion picture *55 Days at Peking* popularized this event.

Your collection includes two fascinating German decorations from World War II, shown on pages 91 and 136. What is the response to these memories from cadets and veterans who visit your museum?

These two decorations were in storage in a German army facility, and the United States Army seized them at the conclusion of the war. I think most people, whether military or civilian, are simply struck by the almost ostentatious nature of these pieces. The Welfare Cross is certainly an example of the Nazi regime's conspicuous display of its power. The Star of the Grand Cross, on the other hand, harkens back to the traditional design of many European orders.

Aztec Club of 1847 Medal
Tiffany & Co.
Origin unknown, c.1870
Gold plated, enamel
L: 3.8 cm; W: 3.5 cm
West Point Museum Collection, United States Military Academy, West Point, New York

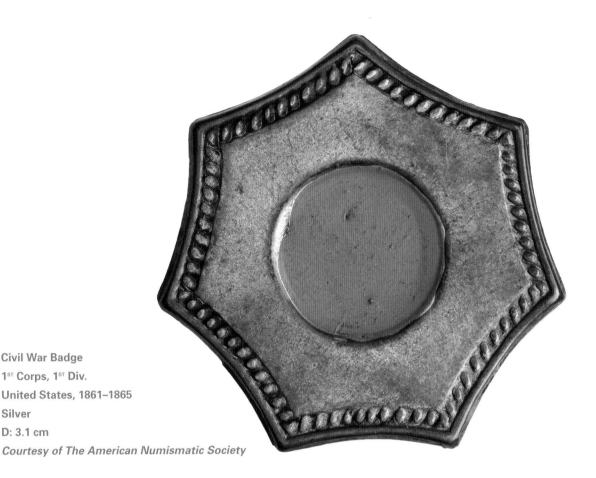

Civil War Badge
1ST Corps, 1ST Div.
United States, 1861–1865
Silver
D: 3.1 cm
Courtesy of The American Numismatic Society

Civil War Badge
16th Corps
United States, 1861–1865
Silver
D: 2.1 cm
Courtesy of The American
Numismatic Society

Page 30 features a Corps badge with a red circle in a seven-pointed star. From the 14TH Corps, also in red, is an acorn-shaped pin with a smaller red acorn imprinted in the center on page 31. From the 12TH and 20TH Corps, page 31, is a star-shaped badge with a smaller blue star in the center. On page 30 is an insignia from the 16TH Corps featuring a round pin with four teardrop shapes cut out in a criss-cross pattern. On page 31 is the badge from the 4TH Corps with a triangle cut out of the center. From the 6TH Corps on page 32 is a circular pin with a cross impressed in the center. The insignia from the 15TH Corps on page 32 is unique in that its square insignia had a raised enameled cartridge that reads "40 Rounds U.S." The most unusual badge

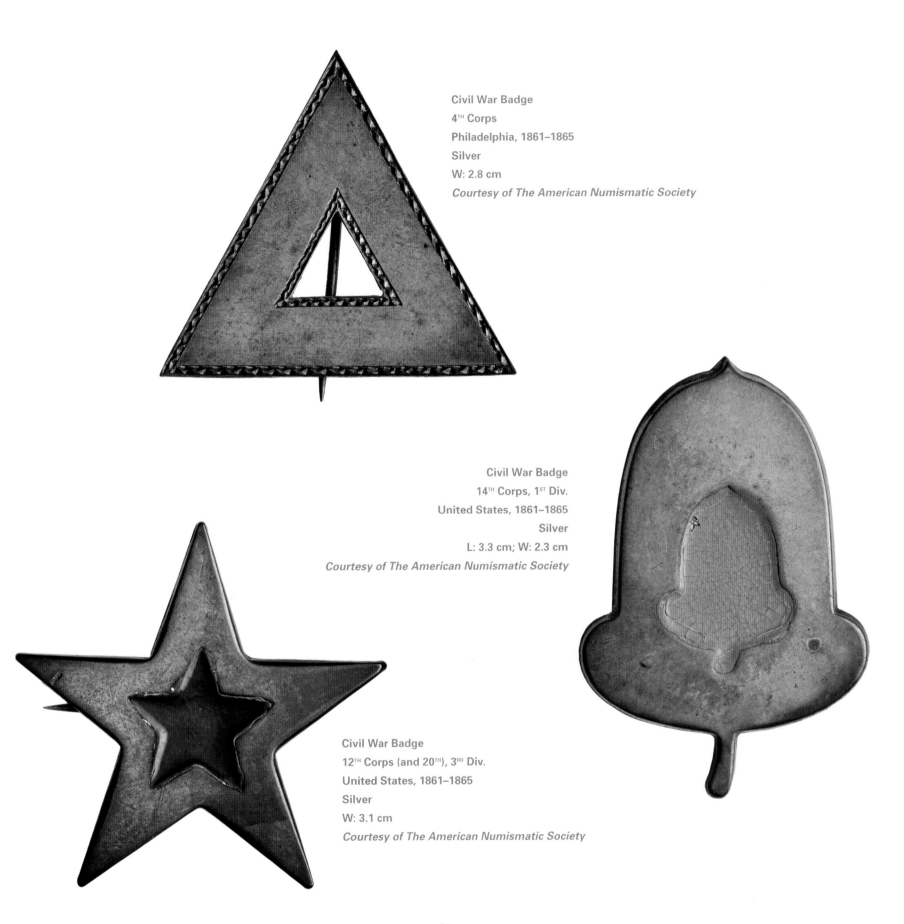

Civil War Badge
4ᵀᴴ Corps
Philadelphia, 1861–1865
Silver
W: 2.8 cm
Courtesy of The American Numismatic Society

Civil War Badge
14ᵀᴴ Corps, 1ˢᵀ Div.
United States, 1861–1865
Silver
L: 3.3 cm; W: 2.3 cm
Courtesy of The American Numismatic Society

Civil War Badge
12ᵀᴴ Corps (and 20ᵀᴴ), 3ᴿᴰ Div.
United States, 1861–1865
Silver
W: 3.1 cm
Courtesy of The American Numismatic Society

Civil War Badge
6TH Corps
United States, 1861–1865
Silver
D: 2.7 cm
*Courtesy of The American
Numismatic Society*

Civil War Badge
15TH Corps
Philadelphia, 1861–1865
Silver
L: 2.9 cm; W: 2.8 cm
*Courtesy of The American
Numismatic Society*

Civil War Badge
19TH Corps
United States, 1861–1865
Silver
L: 3.3 cm; W: 3.2 cm
*Courtesy of The American
Numismatic Society*

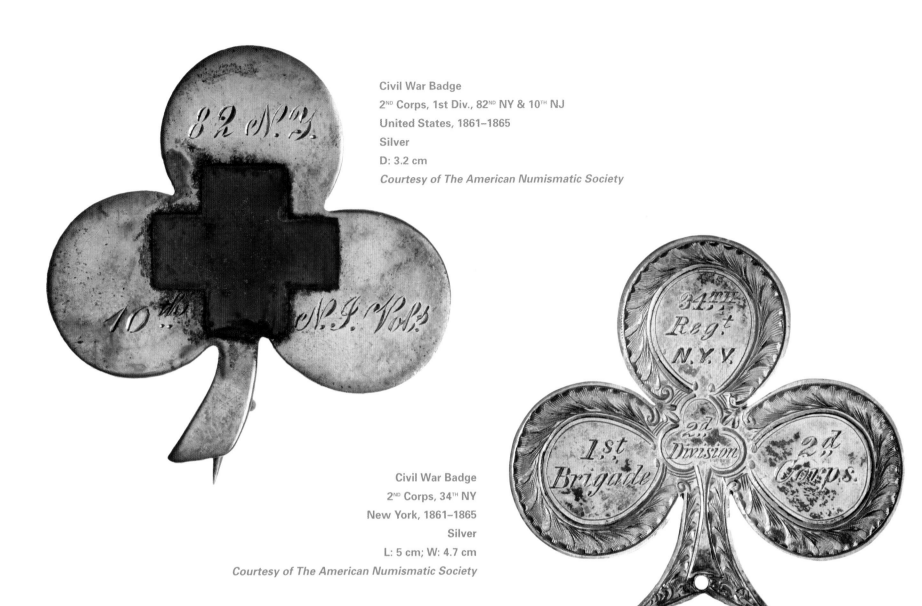

Civil War Badge
2ND Corps, 1st Div., 82ND NY & 10TH NJ
United States, 1861–1865
Silver
D: 3.2 cm
Courtesy of The American Numismatic Society

Civil War Badge
2ND Corps, 34TH NY
New York, 1861–1865
Silver
L: 5 cm; W: 4.7 cm
Courtesy of The American Numismatic Society

is one from the 19TH Corps on page 32 with a cross pattée (a type of cross with arms narrow at the center and broader at the perimeter) with a circular center containing an image of a fortress surrounded by waves with a raised flag. The next badge on page 33 is more ornate as the division is engraved on one of the clover leaves. The most decorative badge is the bordered clover on page 33 for Captain J.O. Scott of the 34TH Regiment, NY and 1ST Brigade 2ND Division, 2ND Corps. The badge designs, like this one of a clover leaf, often reflect the culture of a unit such as Company C of the 116TH Pennsylvania volunteer Infantry of the 2ND Corps, which was part of the famed "Irish Brigade" of mostly Irish Americans. What distinguishes the images on page 34 is their award to "Zouave" soldiers. The term described certain units of Union soldiers who adopted the stylish but fierce military costumes of contemporary French soldiers who simulated the dress of North African warriors.

Civil War Badge
2ND Corps, 164TH NY Corcoran's Zouaves
Philadelphia, 1861–1865
White metal
D: 3.5 cm
Courtesy of The American
  Numismatic Society

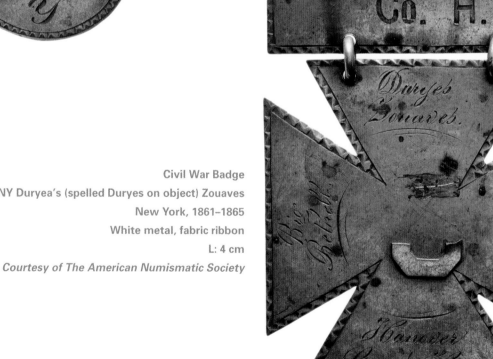

Civil War Badge
5TH NY Duryea's (spelled Duryes on object) Zouaves
New York, 1861–1865
White metal, fabric ribbon
L: 4 cm
Courtesy of The American Numismatic Society

Other Civil War insignia are featured on pages 35 and 36. One of them has, around its border, the "battle list," which is a list of battles the unit fought. During the early part of the Civil War, the cavalry's role was reconnaissance to support the artillery and the infantry. It was not until the Battle of Gettysburg that the reorganized Calvary Corps were assigned to lead the charge. Late in 1864, the Cavalry Corps were accorded the badge on page 37 with its crossed sabers set on top of an oval, within a

Civil War Drum Major Good Conduct Badge
20TH NYM, 21ST NY, 192ND NY
New York, 1861–1865
Silver, fabric ribbon
L: 2.8 cm
Courtesy of The American Numismatic Society

sunburst or "glory." Gouverneur Kemble Warren, one of the Union's most respected generals, was a chief engineer in the Cavalry Corps when it was reorganized. He was known as the hero of Little Round Top at the Battle of Gettysburg where he single-handedly organized the successful defense of the Hill, the smaller of two rocky hills south of Gettysburg, from being reclaimed by the enemy. His Corps badge on page 37 has the crossed sabers of the Cavalry Corps, with the 2-star strap of a Major General. After the war, Warren's sister, Emily Warren Roebling, went on to aid her bed-ridden husband in the completion of the building of the Brooklyn Bridge. Today the bridge has a plaque dedicated to both of them.

Civil War Cavalry Corps
Maker unknown
Origin unknown, c. 1880
Brass, silver, enamel
W: 4.4 cm; H: 1.3 cm / Ribbon: L: 2.5 cm
West Point Museum Collection, United States
Military Academy, West Point, New York

Presentation 5ᵀᴴ Corps Medal of MG Gouverneur K. Warren, USMA 1850
Maker unknown
Origin unknown, 1875
Gold
Badge: L: 5.1 cm / Ribbon: W: 3.8 cm
West Point Museum Collection, United States Military Academy, West Point, New York

37

Indian Wars Campaign Medal of Caleb Henry Carleton, USMA 1859
U.S. Mint
Washington, D.C., Date unknown
Bronze, silk ribbon
L: 6.7 cm / Pendant: D: 3.2 cm
West Point Museum Collection, United States Military Academy,
West Point, New York

Society of the Army of the Cumberland Badge
of Caleb Henry Carleton, USMA 1859
Maker unknown
Origin unknown, Date unknown
Gilt metal, enamel, silk ribbon
L: 7.9 cm; Star W: 4.4 cm
West Point Museum Collection, United States
Military Academy, West Point, New York

Caleb Henry Carleton Served as a Colonel of the 80TH Volunteer Infantry regiment during the Civil War. He then served in the U.S. Army with the 8TH U.S. Cavalry until his retirement as a Brigadier General in 1897.

Veteran's Badge of the 5TH and 14TH Corps of Caleb Henry Carleton, USMA 1859
Maker unknown
Origin unknown, Date unknown
Gilt metal, enamel, silk ribbon
L: 5.1 cm; W: 3.2 cm
West Point Museum Collection, United States Military Academy, West Point, New York

In 1870, the Franco-Prussian War was being waged in Europe. It was the culmination of long tensions between France and Prussia about dominance of German states. Lasting only one year, this war brought about the fall of Napoléon III (son of the brother of Napoléon I), resulting in Germany's annexation of L'Alsace-Lorraine, which France did not reclaim until after WWI. On pages 40 and 41 are oxidized silver pieces with the chained and enameled arms of L'Alsace-Lorraine. The dates on the earrings, 1870 and 1871, recall France's defeat and the loss of her provinces, which is also symbolized by the broken label on the pendant where the word "France" is written (page 41).

Pair of Earrings to commemorate the French loss of L'Alsace-Lorraine
Maker unknown
France, c. 1871
Silver-plated, enamel, gilt copper alloy
H: 5.6 cm; W: 2.3 cm
Victoria and Albert Museum, London

At the dawn of the twentieth century, the British were heavily engaged in South Africa's Boer War, where Winston Churchill first gained recognition as a war correspondent. As successive waves of Boers had migrated away from British rule in the Cape Colony, Britain had recognized two Boer Republics in 1852. The discovery of gold in 1886 escalated tensions in the region, provoking war. After a peace treaty in 1902, the two Republics were absorbed into the British Empire, but the many British concessions resulted in the longest and most costly British war in a century. Patriotic fervor on the home front produced what would become a common signifier: pins for civilian wear, the subject of

Pendant to commemorate the French loss of
    L'Alsace-Lorraine
Maker unknown
France, c. 1871
Silver-plated, enamel, gilt copper alloy
H: 8.9 cm; W: 3.9 cm
Victoria and Albert Museum, London

Windproof Lighter
Alfred Dunhill
Great Britain, 1916
Silver plate, orange cotton cord
L: 5.8 cm; W: 1.9 cm
Alfred Dunhill Museum and Archive

Cannonball Lighter
Joseph Chaumet
Paris, c. 1918
Gold, steel
H: 6 cm; W: 1.4 cm
Collection Chaumet Paris

an amusing book, *Badges*, written by the Keeper of Coins and Medals of the British Museum, Philip Attwood. Curiously, the badge pictured on page 43 was made in the U.S. in the early 1900s, and it recalls Admiral Lord Nelson's famous call to action from the Battle of Trafalgar a century earlier, "England Expects that Every Man will do his duty." Its production in America is potentially due to the mass-production of inexpensive accessories for the first time in the factories of Newark, New Jersey. Also on page 43 is a silver-mounted wooden burlap relic from Lord Nelson's HMS *Victory* ship, which was reconstructed about 1805.

The Great War, or World War I, ironically became known as "The War to End All Wars." The extreme and brutal conditions were surpassed in horror less than three decades later:

42

Relic from Lord Nelson's HMS *Victory* Ship
Maker unknown
England, 1798–1806
Silver, mounted wood, burlap
L: 8.9 cm
Historical Design Inc.

" England expects every man to do his duty "

Boer War Badge—"England expects . . ."
Whitehead & Hoag
Newark, c. 1900
Base metal, celluloid, paper
D without pin: 2.2 cm
The British Museum

Tank Wristwatch
Cartier
Paris, 1920
Platinum, sapphire cabochon, leather strap
Case: L: 2.96 cm; W: 2.3 cm
Cartier Collection

poison gas attacks, modernized artillery and machine guns, and regiments of soldiers confined to trenches for months on end. Smoking was one of a soldier's few pleasures, and the prevalent diversion necessitated lighters. Alfred Dunhill created the windproof lighter on page 42, to help deal with the miseries of the trenches. Dunhill inherited his father's saddlery business, but responded to the demand for automobiles by developing a line of accessories called Dunhill's Motorities.

Chaumet, the classic French firm founded in 1780 and jeweler to Napoléon Bonaparte, created the lighter in gold and steel on page 42, an allusion to the hand grenades and modified artillery shells utilized by infantry. As homage to the tank commanders who defended France, Louis Cartier originally designed the still contemporary "Tank Watch" on page 44. The design's inspiration came from the Renault tanks which Cartier saw in action on the Western Front. Louis Cartier presented the prototype of the watch in 1917 to General John Pershing,

Fabergé Eagle Trays
Fabergé
Russia, c. 1914
Silver, brass, copper
D: 10.8 cm each
Courtesy of A La Vieille Russie

Commander of the American Expeditionary Force in Europe.

According to *International Watch Magazine*, "WWI marked the emergence of the wristwatch as a piece of the military kit. Troops on all sides found it an encumbrance to unbutton a heavy coat to check pocket watches. These new wristwatches were typically 13-ligne with luminous numerals and hands, enameled dial, wire-strap lugs, and fitted with protective grills. They were made by Girard-Perregaux, Movado, Waltham, Elgin,

Solerex, and Ingersoll [now Timex] and were referred to as 'Soldier' watches in their ads to the general public."

Peter Carl Fabergé, best known for his exquisite eggs, created the three eagle ashtrays on page 45. Each was made during WWI, featuring a large Russian Imperial Eagle, the inscription "War 1914," and Fabergé's signature. The silver piece is the original, whereas those in copper and brass were made to express austerity by the use of lesser materials. The Russian losses

Earrings
Tiffany & Co.
United States, c. 1941
14k gold
L: 1.6 cm; W: 1.9 cm; D: 1.6 cm
Tiffany & Co. Archives

in WWI were devastating; it is estimated that over a million Russians were killed before Russia withdrew its forces under terms of the Treaty of Versailles. Hugely unpopular in Russia, the Czar's War, which crippled the economy and destroyed his remaining support with the population, paved the way for the Russian Revolution.

During the 1920s and 1930s, gangsters popularized the use of the Tommy Gun, or semi-automatic machine gun. However, criminal usage

Winston Churchill as
    Prime Minister
Horton
Great Britain, 1940
Imperial War Museum

was small compared to the number of soldiers shouldering the gun in the Second World War. On page 46 is a photo of Winston Churchill with

a 1928 Thompson model. Between 1940 and the end of WWII, the British ordered over 105,000 guns, and by 1944 over 1.2 million were being produced annually. John Thompson, who invented the Tommy Gun, graduated from West Point, class of 1882, served in the Spanish-American War, and during WWI was promoted to Brigadier General, responsible for the supply of small arms and ammunition to the Allied Expeditionary Force in France. His company was called the Auto-Ordnance Company. On page 47 is a Tiffany & Co. Tommy Gun pin. According to the Director of the Tiffany & Co. Archives, Annamarie Sandecki, the Auto Ordnance Corps ordered these machine guns in 1947 as mounts for bill clips.

Another inspiration from war was the 1944 Tiffany gold bracelet on page 50, resembling the chain link treads of tank tracks; gold, clunky jewelry was all the rage in the early 1940s. Tiffany also created airplane earrings on page 46 in the shape of an American DC-3 bomber, with moveable wing propellers.

The Spitfire, an important WWII fighter plane, was the victim of severe production problems during its fabrication, causing a confrontation between the British Air Ministry and the Vickers Armstrong Aircraft Company. Lord Beaverbrook was a Canadian-British politician and newspaper publisher. He founded the *Sunday* and then the *Daily Express*. In 1940 Winston Churchill appointed him Minister of Aircraft Production. Severe delays resulted in Lord Beaverbrook assuming control of the

Vickers Armstrong factory in Southampton, which was tasked to produce 10 complete Spitfires by the end of June, 1940. Successful completion of the project target was commemorated with gifts of the Alfred Dunhill lighter and ashtray pictured on page 48 to the builders. During the war, Dunhill also produced the service lighters on page 49.

A masterpiece of a war tribute is shown on page 51. This onyx and nephrite eight-day, five time-zone desk clock was a Christmas gift to

Franklin Roosevelt on December 23, 1943, from Pierre Cartier, who, during the War, had to shift his major production facilities away from Paris. "The hour of victory" dedication reflected growing optimism in the West in 1943, as the allies entered Naples on October 1ST, the Russians recaptured Kiev on November 6TH, and the British bombed Berlin on November 18TH. This progression of events led to the Teheran Conference on November 28TH, where Roosevelt, Churchill, and Stalin convened to discuss the

invasion plans which resulted in D-Day. In addition to the main time zone on the clock, note the other four time zones where Allied soldiers were deployed: London-Paris; Berlin-Rome; San Francisco; and Tokyo. Because Paris had converted to the Central European time-zone with Berlin in 1940, Cartier's pairing of Paris and London cleverly implied the forthcoming

liberation of the Nazi-occupied French capital. The workmanship is extraordinary: each time zone can be set separately and yet all of the minutes advance in unison.

F.D.R. kept this piece in his library in Hyde Park, New York in its red leather presentation case, which boasted a gold-tooled border with "F.D.R." engraved on it. "The F.D.R. Cartier

48

Service Lighter
Alfred Dunhill
United States, 1944–1945
Steel, aluminum
L: 6 cm; W: 2 cm
Alfred Dunhill Museum and Archive

Service Lighter
Alfred Dunhill
United States, 1944–1945
Steel, aluminum
L: 6 cm; W: 2 cm
Alfred Dunhill Museum and Archive

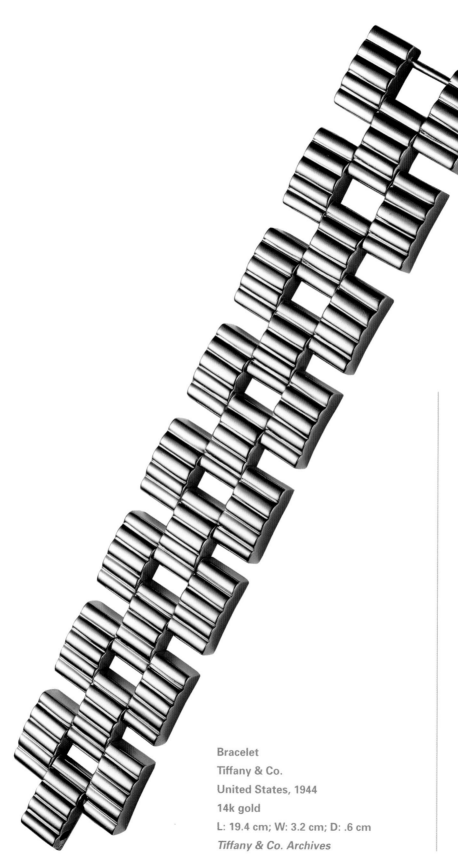

Bracelet
Tiffany & Co.
United States, 1944
14k gold
L: 19.4 cm; W: 3.2 cm; D: .6 cm
Tiffany & Co. Archives

Victory Clock is remarkable for its design and history," says Aaron Rich, Vice President and head of watches for Sotheby's New York. "Its Art Deco lines are masculine and bold. The ability to mix design with elaborate technical clock-making is something that always set Cartier apart from other makers. However the idea that President Roosevelt might have seen the time in all the theatres of the War in one glance is breathtaking." F.D.R. was moved to thank Cartier for the gift by concluding: "Soon, very soon, I hope that Paris will resume her place among the free capitals of the world."

The F.D.R. Cartier Victory Clock
Cartier
New York, 1930; presented to F.D.R. 1943
Silver, ebonite, enamel, nephrite
H: 22 cm; W: 20 cm; D: 11 cm
Private Collection

VALOR

The Patton family history also provides us an insight into the meaning of valor. A friend of George Patton wanted a photo of Patton in full military dress. On this occasion Patton displayed his Légion d'honneur, his Order of the British Empire (OBE), and the Luxembourg Croix de Guerre with ribbons specially made in London. Patton received two Distinguished Service Crosses, a Bronze Star, a Purple Heart, and two French Liberation Medals from Metz for World War I and World War II (see page 53). Victory was all-important to Patton, and as a youth he often staged mock ancient battles, with the young Patton always emerging as the victor. His mother was curious about the source of his military knowledge. "Oh Mother," Patton supposedly said, "I was there." Stories about Patton reveal a man who was so militarily minded he may well have lived a former life at the time of the Roman Empire.

During the Roman Empire, the award of medals for valor developed as a privilege limited to officers in the military. It was not until the eighteenth century that such recognitions were

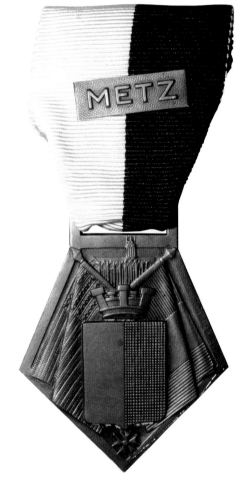

made available to their troops as well, starting in the Americas at the time of the American Revolution; governments in Europe did not democratize the process until later.

An example of the oldest U.S. medal for valor, the Fidelity Medallion, dates back to 1780 and can be seen on page 54. This particular medal was awarded to three soldiers who helped capture British Army Major General André, the Commander in Arms of American traitor Benedict Arnold. On the front is a shield and wreath inscribed "FIDELITY." On the reverse are two thistle plants, surrounded by the words "VINCENT AMOR PATRIÆ" ("Love of Country Conquers"). The medal was not struck, but was finished in *repoussé*, a technique inherited from the ancient Middle East. *Repoussé* (from the French meaning "pushed up") forms a raised design. The dedication reads: "Presented by Congress to John Paulding for the Capture of Major André, Sept. 26TH 1780." The New York Historical Society had in their possession two of

Capture of André Medal
Maker unknown
United States, 1780
Silver
L: 6.2 cm; W: 4.2 cm
Courtesy of The American Numismatic Society

the three original medals—those awarded to John Paulding and David Williams—but both of these were stolen from a locked exhibition showcase in 1976. It is believed that the example from the American Numismatic Society, featured on page 54, is a copy that was made shortly after the original Paulding medal was struck.

The Society of the Cincinnati was the earliest society commemorating valor in the service of General Washington. Established on May 13, 1783 by George Washington's officers, the Society's objectives were to "preserve the rights suddenly won, promote the continuing union of the states, and to assist the members in need." One of the earliest Cincinnati medals, on page 56 belonged to Henry Dearborn. Dearborn was trained as a physician and joined George Washington's army at Valley Forge as a Lieu-

tenant-Colonel. In 1801, he became Secretary of War under President Thomas Jefferson, and in 1812 was appointed by President James Madison as Senior Major General of the U.S. Army. It was during the War of 1812 that Dearborn wanted to invade Canada, but it never happened. His failure to act resulted in his losing his military command. It is believed that Dearborn wore this medal at Washington's funeral.

One exceptional Cincinnati medal, owned by la Fondation Josée et René de Chambrun, was presented to Marie-Joseph Paul Yves Roch Gilbert du Motier, the Marquis de Lafayette, by Washington for his service as a general in the Continental Army and is shown on page 57. It was designed by Major Pierre L'Enfant, a French officer who joined the American Army in 1777 and later planned and designed the city of

Washington, D.C., and the medal was created by Duvall Francastel and associated firms in Paris. L'Enfant first awarded officers the medal in 1784. The Society is named after the Roman hero Cincinnatus who on the front of the decoration is abandoning his plough and taking up the sword and on the back is acknowledging a subject. Another version of the medal reflects the Society's motto, "*Omnia relinquit servare Republicam*" ("He relinquished everything to preserve the Republic"). The original ribbon, with its blue and white colors, symbolizes the bond between the U.S. and France. In fact, these earlier medals were made in France, but later medals, like the one on page 9, were made in the U.S. and forged in stamped metal.

After a successful military stint in the U.S., Lafayette returned to France in 1779, was

Society of the Cincinnati Order Badge
Society of the Cincinnati
United States, c. 1784
Gold, enamel
L: 12.2 cm
Courtesy of The American Numismatic Society

promoted to Major General in the French Army, and eventually awarded command of the Paris National Guard, which is similar to the U.S. National Guard. The National Guard played an important role after the abolition of the monarchy on September 21, 1792, when it forced the wishes of the revolutionaries upon the French National Assembly. A modern jeweled emblem of the National Guard is the tri-color cockade, a circular symbol usually worn on a hat, on page 58, crafted by Cartier in 1918. Lafayette introduced the tri-color cockade to symbolize new order in France. Originally the cockade was blue and red, the symbol of the royals. When the Bastille fell in 1789, Lafayette was responsible for the security of Louis XVI—it was Lafayette who took the royal family onto the balcony of the King's apartments to reason with the crowds who were storming their palace at Versailles. The Order

Washington-Marquis de Lafayette Order of the Society of the Cincinnati (front)
Attributed to Duval and Francastel and associated firms
Paris, 1783–1784
Gold, enamel, silk ribbon
L: 3.8 cm; W: 2.6 cm
L with ribbon and clasp: 14 cm
Fondation Josée et René de Chambrun

Washington-Marquis de Lafayette Order of the Society
of the Cincinnati (back)

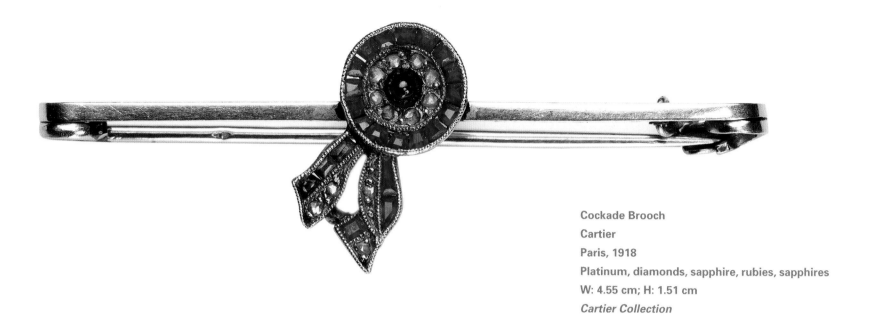

Cockade Brooch
Cartier
Paris, 1918
Platinum, diamonds, sapphire, rubies, sapphires
W: 4.55 cm; H: 1.51 cm
Cartier Collection

of the Saint-Louis is pictured on page 17. It was given to exceptional officers and was the first decoration accorded to non-nobles. The front of the decoration consists of a portrait of Saint Louis surrounded by the words LUD(OVICUS) M(AGNUS) IN(STITUIT) 1693, "Louis the Great Instituted in 1693." Lafayette, who was quite outspoken in his opinions, declared to George Washington, "I would have never drawn my sword in the cause of America if I could have conceived thereby that I was founding a land of slavery." The bond between Washington and Lafayette is eloquently expressed by John Quincy Adams in his 1825

farewell address to Lafayette in Washington, D.C. "We shall look upon you always as belonging to us, during the whole of your life, and as belonging to our children after us. You are ours by that more than patriotic self-devotion with which you flew to the aid of our fathers at the crisis of our fate; ours by that unshaken gratitude for your services which is a precious portion of our inheritance; ours by that tie of love, stronger than death, which has linked your name for the endless ages of time with the name of Washington."

In 1804 Napoléon crowned himself Emperor of France. Six years later he divorced his

first wife, Josephine, as she could not produce any heirs, and married Marie-Louise, Archduchess of Austria, a great-niece of Marie Antoinette. On page 5 is an extraordinary Order of the Iron Crown, produced in 1805 by François-Regnault Nitot. Napoléon created the Iron Crown in 1805. He took the name from the Iron Crown of Lombardy, a crown featuring a nail, allegedly from Jesus' cross. The Lombardy Crown was used in Charlemagne's coronation. When Napoléon conquered Italy and called himself King of Italy, he crowned himself with the original Lombardy Iron Crown which was made for Theodelina of Lombardy in 628. When Napoléon was defeated

Snuffbox with Crowned Monogram of Napoléon I
Marie-Etienne Nitot, Etienne-Lucien Blerzy
Paris, 1807–1808
Gold, diamonds
L: 7.5 cm; W: 5.5 cm; D: 1.8 cm
Ledoux Napoléon Art Collection

Snuffbox with Crowned Monogram of Napoléon I
(side detail)

Portrait Miniature of
Napoléon's Son, King
of Rome, Francois-
Joseph-Charles
Miniature attributed to
Nicolas Jacques
France, 1814–1815
Ivory
L: 5.7 cm; W: 4 cm
*Ledoux Napoléon Art
Collection*

Portrait Miniature of
Napoléon's Wife,
Empress Marie-Louise
Miniature attributed to
Nicolas Jacques
France, 1814–1815
Ivory
L: 5.7 cm; W: 4 cm
*Ledoux Napoléon Art
Collection*

Secret Snuffbox with Portrait of Napoléon I
Miniature attributed to Nicolas Jacques; Goldsmith: Gabriel-Raoul Morel
France, 1814–1815
Gold, ivory
Dimensions of Box: L: 8.2 cm; W: 5.6 cm; H: 2.2 cm
Dimensions of Miniature: L: 4.9 cm; W: 3.5 cm
Ledoux Napoléon Art Collection

at Waterloo in 1815, the French Iron Crown ceased to exist but was still worn by the Emperor of Austria and Austria-Hungary until 1918. This jewel was presented to Napoléon on the occasion of his wedding to Marie-Louise.

This piece is comprised of 202 diamonds with ruby and sapphire, gold, and enamel. The inscription at the bottom reads *"Dío me la diede gauí a chí la tocca"* or "God gave it to me, mind the one who touches it." The center of the award consists of an oval medallion, decorated with a golden bust of the French emperor. Another Nitot jewel is a diamond and gold snuff box featured on page 59 that belonged to Napoléon. Snuff boxes contained ground tobacco that was inhaled or snuffed through the nose, which was the fashionable habit at that time. Napoléon also commissioned miniature portraitist Jean-Baptiste Isabey, a pupil of Jacques-Louis David, to create his image wearing the Légion d'honneur, which was the center painting on the gold snuff box on page 61. Also on page 60 is a unique gold snuff box with portraits of Napoléon, his

wife, and his son. Francois-Regnault Nitot's father was the founder of Chaumet, the company Napoléon charged with making jewelry, of which the diminutive Napoléon was very fond, enjoying its symbolism of power and prestige.

Snuffbox with Portrait of Napoléon I
Miniature: Jean-Baptiste Isabey;
    Jeweler: Marguerite
Paris, 1806
Gold, enamel, miniature
Dimensions of Box: L: 8.5 cm; W: 6 cm; D: 2 cm
Dimensions of Miniature: L: 5.4 cm; W: 3.5 cm
Ledoux Napoléon Art Collection

Bruno Ledoux

Bruno Ledoux manages important real estate and financial businesses in Paris. He is also active in the fields of entertainment, film industry, and television. His passion led him to create one of the world's most important collections of historical objects from Napoléon and his Imperial reign and from the era of the French Revolution.

Why do historians credit Napoléon as one of the greatest military heroes?

In your question, there are three important words: hero, military, and history. The word "hero" refers to an epic; "military" to an art whose mastery was that of a genius; and "history" to the importance of Napoléon's work. Napoléon was the personification of these three aspects, found only in few great figures, like Caesar, Alexander, and Hannibal.

The epic story of Napoléon tells how he conquered faraway lands. It is the adventure of a lonely man who believed in his dreams and let his steps be guided by the quest. He is Egypt; he is the Coronation.

The military art of Napoléon is great: more than forty victories, almost always outnumbered against an allied Europe. He devised a new military strategy, where time is the key for victory, based on a mathematical analysis of data and men, a strategy that grounded modern warfare.

History, political and military, also reveals Napoléon's legal masterwork. The result is that of a leader who integrated the first European political arena, dominated and administered by France. He introduced the Age of Enlightenment, the new ideas of the 1789 Revolution, and the declaration of the Rights of Man and of the citizen.

Finally, it is above all an incredible belief in one's own destiny: an infinite desire to make it a part of history, something never realized on this scale and in such a short time of barely twenty years. During his lifetime, Napoléon was fully aware of his destiny. Facing the future, he won his last victory against eternity, Sainte-Hélène, where he was exiled by the British.

What story about Napoléon would give us a better picture of the man and the soldier?

As a man it is Sainte-Hélène, where he rewrites his own life and conducts his last battle: a spiritual one, with no army, not against an enemy but against time. It is the birth of the myth.

As a soldier, it is the victory of Austerlitz. Austerlitz is considered one of the greatest battles of Napoléon. On that occasion he fought against the Russian Army, under the command of General Kutusov. The Emperor maneuvered in order to force the enemy to carry out his own battle plans and to follow his own strategy. Napoléon was victorious on the anniversary of his coronation, December 2, 1805.

What was the unique concept of the Napoléonic Code?

Bonaparte wished to unify Europe with all enjoying the same rights. As renewing ideas from the 1789 revolution, he wanted to establish clear rules that would ensure each citizen with a minimum of civil liberty. It was, therefore, an effort to unify the Revolution and the "Ancien Régime." The Civil Code is founded on promoting secularism. Marriage is confirmed as a civil act, and not only a sacrament under religious authority. Real estate property becomes personal. The freedom to work is absolute. The code has been used by many countries, and is still a cornerstone of French civil law.

What distinguished Napoléon's strategy of war from the great generals who succeeded him?

Napoléon invented the "movement war" where the time factor is decisive. He focused his strengths on a specific spot, generally at the center of the enemy's position. He attacked this center point to divide the enemy's army into two parts, marshalling all his forces against one side, crushing it, and then attacking the other. That way, one against two, he won the battle. All his actions were based on the relation of space and time.

European allied armies were still using the eighteenth century's war strategies. They spread their armies along a great frontline and maneuvered slowly. When motion and time become the critical factors, logistics are the main constraint. Hence, Napoléon left nothing to chance, attending to everything from the clothing of the simple soldier to the overall strategy. Any error in the general plan at any level could jeopardize the system and compromise victory.

Napoléon possessed extraordinary taste in objects such as jewels and weaponry. How did it come about? Was he born with it or was it taught to him?

Napoléon is a man from modest social background who became an emperor. He suffered from a complex of his origins, especially when dealing with the Divine Right monarchy. He naturally became interested in anything that could prove his power, both at social and military levels.

Like the great kings and patrons of the history of France, Francois 1er or Louis XIV, he understood the value of arts for France to affirm its European influence. Such artistic influence would greatly benefit France, and Napoléon, in the quest for European supremacy and also would maintain his influence in the years to come.

Creator of a new nobility, Napoléon granted privileges, titles, and functions, and offered luxurious gifts as evidence of his power and legitimacy. The same strategy was developed to affirm his status before European courts. Napoléon gathered around him the best artists to create these gifts: David for painting; Percier and Fontaine for architecture; Nitot for jewelry; Biennais for gold, silver and marquetery; Jacob-Desmalter for cabinetry; Sèvres for porcelains; and Bozérian for bindings. Napoléon learned from his close relationship with artists, and through Empress Josephine who knew about real refinement and good taste, how to manage his image and the aura of France.

In the 1840s and 1850s in the United States, many German and Irish immigrants arrived in Eastern cities like New York, Boston, and Baltimore. In a xenophobic response, movements started to oppose Catholics, Jews, and other immigrants. Activists started forming secret societies, and when asked about their members and origins, claimed they "knew nothing," accounting for the name of the Know Nothing Party of the 1840s, which was originally named the Native American party. A badge from the American Volunteers Group, on page 64, displays the Group's anti-immigrant slogan, originally a quote from George Washington, "Place None but Americans on Guard." On the other side is an inscription: "Awarded to Corp W. H. Welch by Co A, American Volunteers for his superior skills in military drill, Brooklyn May 29TH 1856." There

Society of American Volunteers Badge
Society of American Volunteers
New York, 1856
Silver
L: 8.1 cm; W: 5.6 cm
Courtesy of The American Numismatic Society

were hundreds of these groups at the time, but their popularity waned thereafter.

Today, the highest and most important American award for valor in combat remains the Medal of Honor, authorized by President Abraham Lincoln in 1861. According to official citations, "The deed of the person must be proved by incontestable evidence of at least two eyewitnesses; it must be so outstanding that it clearly distinguishes gallantry beyond the call of duty from lesser forms of bravery; it must involve risk of life; and it must be the type of deed, if he had not done it, would not subject him to any justified criticism." When asked why he never received a Medal of Honor, General Patton claimed that all the witnesses were killed. One of the earliest, on page 65, was awarded in 1862 to Private James Webb, Company F, 5TH NY Infantry, for gallantry at Bull Run, Virginia during the Civil War. As a result of the defeat of the North at Bull Run, President Lincoln signed a bill providing 500,000 more enlisted men.

Medal of Honor, U.S. Military Decoration
Civil War, Army Issue
United States, 1862
Bronze
L: 13 cm
Courtesy of The American Numismatic Society

Webb's Medal of Honor is typical of the earliest Army awards; its forefront features an eagle perched on a bar with a suspended star. The ribbon, however, is the later 1896 version of the medal. The 1862 ribbon is the same as that on the Navy Medal of Honor on page 66, "given for personal valor to James H. Lee, Seaman of the USS *Kearsarge*, Destruction of the *Alabama*, July 19, 1864." The *Alabama* was the focus of one of the most important naval battles of the War because the Confederate raider sunk over $10 million in

Davis Guards Sabine Pass Medal
Confederate States of America
Houston, 1863
Silver
D: 3.7 cm
*Courtesy of The American Numismatic
    Society*

Northern ships and supplies. It is interesting to note that the battle took place off Cherbourg, France. The British-built *Alabama* was in the area searching for supplies. Manet painted an oil of the fight which is now at the Philadelphia Museum of Art. Note the difference between the Navy and Army medals. The Navy medal uses an anchor to support the medal rather than the eagle in the Army version.

The Civil War also produced an important award called the Davis Guard Medal for the Defense of Sabine Pass. The medal shown on page 67 was awarded to Lt. Richard Dowling, on September 8, 1863. On the front is a Maltese Cross, with the letters "DG" for Davis Guard. The medal was created from a Mexican silver peso, smoothed off, and engraved on each side. The victory was important to the Confederacy because it halted the invasion by the Union into Texas along the Sabine River. Dowling was known for his armament skill: when a Union boat tried to enter the Sabine River, Dowling's attacks from above forced the ship to retreat. Dowling captured more than 350 Union soldiers.

Historically, Marshal is the highest rank above a full General in many military organizations. French aristocracy established the rank, Maréchal de France, which today is not a military rank but a distinction given to generals of exceptional achievement. French marshals have included Maréchal Ferdinand Foch—WWI, Maréchal Alphonse Juin—WWI, and Maréchal Philippe Pétain, who acquired the rank in WWI

and regained the title in WWII as Head of State from the Germans in occupied France. The British had theirs too: Field Marshal Bernard Montgomery commanded British forces during World War II. By contrast, the rank of Field Marshal did not exist in the U.S. military, which used variations of General to express the highest rank. General John J. Pershing was General of the Armies in WWI. General George Marshall, General Dwight D. Eisenhower, and General

Alphonse Juin, born in French Algeria fought in both World War I and World War II. In 1952 Général Juin was promoted to Maréchal of France.

Maréchal Juin's Distinguished Services Medal
Maker unknown
United States, twentieth century
Metal, textile
L: 10 cm; W: 4 cm
Musée de l'Armée

Douglas MacArthur were five-star generals in command of their theatres of war in WWII. It is noteworthy that these three comrades in arms commanded only the world's seventeenth-largest army at the commencement of hostilities in 1940.

On page 69 are General Eisenhower's sterling silver five-star cluster and his Shield of the Army. Dwight D. Eisenhower and George S. Patton served together in the Tank Corps during WWI, and according to Merle Miller in *Ike the Soldier*, Patton would both "delight and dismay him for the rest of his life," remaining friends until Patton's death in 1945. Anne Eisenhower, granddaughter of President Eisenhower observes, "When my grandfather retired from the Presidency, he preferred to be addressed as General Eisenhower, not President Eisenhower. He was proudest of his military title." Eisenhower was the commander of the Allies landing in North Africa in 1942, and in 1944 on D-Day he was the Supreme Commander of the Allies invading France.

The baton marks a Field Marshal's symbol of rank. The name derives from the French word for "stick," or earlier the Latin *bastum* for "stout staff." The baton was originally the symbol of a Roman general, and Napoléon I modeled the batons after this. We have three exceptional examples. On page 70 is a baton that belonged to German Emperor Wilhelm I, who achieved the unification of Germany and established the German Empire. His baton, for his success in the Sckleswig-Holstein War of 1864, is 19½ inches long and 1½ inches wide with a triple purple velvet material with superimposed oak leaves, from Germany's national tree. Gold caps enclose each end.

Another baton, shown on page 71 is a masterpiece from the Musée de l'Armée in Paris. It was presented to Maréchal Ferdinand Foch in 1920 when he became an honorary member of the Knights of Columbus. In 1882 in Connecticut, Father Michael J. McGivney chartered the Knights of Columbus, now the largest Catholic organization in the world. Its

Field Marshal's Baton of Wilhelm I of Germany
Maker unknown
Assumed Prussian origin, c. 1864
Purple velvet, metallic embroidery, gold caps
L: 50.2 cm; D: 3.8 cm
West Point Museum Collection, United States
Military Academy, West Point, New York

Baton of Maréchal Foch
Tiffany & Co.
United States, c. 1920
Gold, sapphires, lapis-lazuli, copper, enamel
L: 52 cm; D: 5.5 cm
Musée de l'Armée

Baton of Maréchal Foch (detail)

mission was to offer financial and educational aid to its members—men who were eighteen years and older and practicing Catholics. Foch served as General of the French Army during WWI. The Knights of Columbus commissioned Tiffany to make the baton with American ingredients: gold from California, lapis lazuli from Oregon, sapphires from Montana, and copper from Colorado. In the deep-blue enamel are set gold stars bearing the name of each state. The star at the top is marked "Cuba" and made of American gin nickel. The baton is 20½ inches long, and the base is embossed in gold with Foch's capital victories: Metz, Strasbourg. Above this in gold on red copper is "*Terror Belli, Decus Pacis*" or "Terrible in War, Gentle in Peace," with the inscription "Maréchal Ferdinand Foch 1914–1919," surrounded by the golden arms of France, the U.S.,

Baton of Field Marshal Allenby (detail)

Lorraine's dual cross, and the arms of the Knights of Columbus. Some 250 Knights of Columbus came to Metz to unveil and dedicate a statue to Lafayette and present the baton to Foch. The Knights of Columbus specifically chose Metz for the ceremony, as this was the site of Lafayette's French military training before he departed France to aid Washington in the American Revolution. It is also the site where the Germans retreated as French and American armies liberated the city.

One of the more colorful and highly decorated British Field Marshals during WWI was

Baton of Field Marshal Allenby
Garrard & Co. Ltd.
London, 1919
Gold, silver gilt, velvet
L: 35.5 cm; D (max): 5.3 cm
Imperial War Museum (UNI 12184)

FROM
His Majesty
GEORGE V
King
OF THE
UNITED KINGDOM
OF
GREAT BRITAIN AND IRELAND
TO
FIELD MARSHAL
SIR EDMUND HENRY
HYNMAN ALLENBY
G.C.B., G.C.M.G.
1919

Badge of a Knight Grand Cross of the Most Distinguished Order of St. Michael and St. George (GCMG)
Awarded to Field Marshal Edmund Allenby
Garrard & Co. Ltd.
London, awarded 1918
Silver gilt, enamels
L: 11.7 cm; W: 7.2 cm
Imperial War Museum (OMD 1366)

Field Marshal Edmund Allenby, 1ST Viscount Allenby who was also known as "Bloody Bull," earning this nickname because of his violent temper. During WWI he was made Comander-in-Chief of the Egyptian Expeditionary Force and supported T.E. Lawrence (Lawrence of Arabia) to the tune of £200,000 a month in an attempt to control the Arabs. Allenby's medals and baton are housed in the Imperial War Museum's collections and are shown on pages 72 through 81. By 1917 Allenby moved upwards from Egypt and captured Jerusalem. It is interesting that Allenby dismounted his horse and entered by foot out of respect for Jerusalem as a holy city.

Breast Star of the Order of Al Nahda (Hejaz)
Awarded to Field Marshal Edmund Allenby
Maker unknown
Mecca, awarded 1920
Gold, silver, silver gilt, brilliants
D (max): 8.2 cm
Imperial War Museum (OMD 419b)

Breast Star of the Order of the Sardar U Allah
Awarded to Field Marshal Edmund Allenby
Maker unknown
Afghanistan, c. 1920
Silver gilt
D (max): 9 cm
Imperial War Museum (OMD 426b)

Breast Star of the Order of Mohammed Ali
Awarded to Field Marshal Edmund Allenby
Maker unknown
Egypt, c. 1920
Silver gilt, enamels
D (max): 9 cm
Imperial War Museum (OMD 409b)

Grand Cordon (Breast Star) of the Order of the Nile

Awarded to Field Marshal Edmund Allenby

Maker unknown

Egypt, c. 1920

Silver gilt, enamel

D (max): 10.5 cm

Imperial War Museum (OMD 407b)

Badge of a Knight Grand Cross of the Royal
  Victorian Order (GCVO)
Awarded to Field Marshal Edmund Allenby
Maker unknown
United Kingdom, awarded 1934
Silver gilt, enamel
L: 9 cm; W: 7.5 cm
Imperial War Museum (OMD 1367)

Collar of a Knight Grand Cross of the Most Distinguished
  Order of St. Michael and St. George (GCMG)
Awarded to Field Marshal Edmund Allenby
Garrard & Co. Ltd.
London, awarded 1918
Silver gilt, enamel
L: 28 cm; W: 4 cm
Imperial War Museum (OMD 5882)

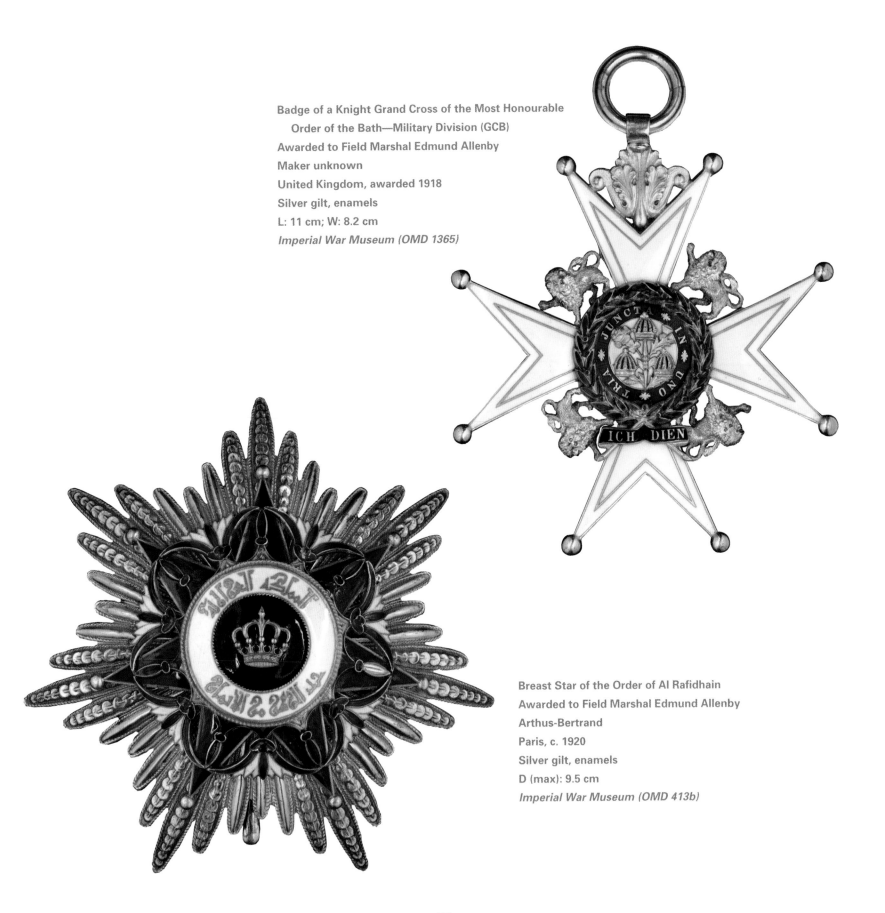

Badge of a Knight Grand Cross of the Most Honourable
   Order of the Bath—Military Division (GCB)
Awarded to Field Marshal Edmund Allenby
Maker unknown
United Kingdom, awarded 1918
Silver gilt, enamels
L: 11 cm; W: 8.2 cm
Imperial War Museum (OMD 1365)

Breast Star of the Order of Al Rafidhain
Awarded to Field Marshal Edmund Allenby
Arthus-Bertrand
Paris, c. 1920
Silver gilt, enamels
D (max): 9.5 cm
Imperial War Museum (OMD 413b)

Breast Star of the Order of the Striped Tiger
Awarded to Field Marshal Edmund Allenby
Maker unknown, marked on reverse
China, c. 1920
Silver gilt, enamels
D (max): 10 cm
Imperial War Museum (OMD 408b)

Breast Star of the Order of the Rising Sun
Awarded to Field Marshal Edmund Allenby
Maker unknown, marked on reverse
Japan, 1921
Silver gilt, enamels
D (max): 9 cm
Imperial War Museum (OMD 416b)

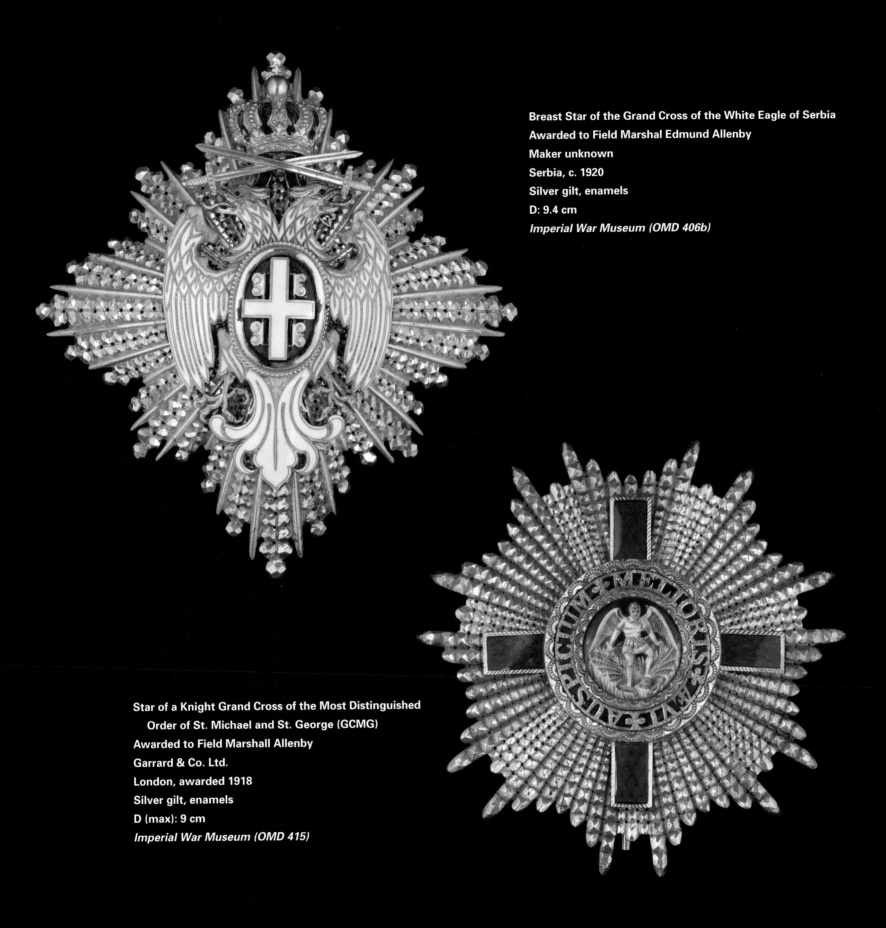

Breast Star of the Grand Cross of the White Eagle of Serbia
Awarded to Field Marshal Edmund Allenby
Maker unknown
Serbia, c. 1920
Silver gilt, enamels
D: 9.4 cm
Imperial War Museum (OMD 406b)

Star of a Knight Grand Cross of the Most Distinguished
    Order of St. Michael and St. George (GCMG)
Awarded to Field Marshall Allenby
Garrard & Co. Ltd.
London, awarded 1918
Silver gilt, enamels
D (max): 9 cm
Imperial War Museum (OMD 415)

Fergus Read

Fergus Read heads the Department of Collections Access of the Imperial War Museum (IWM), based in London. His team curates the museum's three-dimensional items except for sculpture, aircraft, and vehicles. This large collection includes the Orders, Decorations and Medals of Winston Churchill, Field Marshal Montgomery, and other notables. He took his Master's Degree in Museum Studies at Leicester University and worked extensively with military and social history collections across the UK before joining the IWM in 2003.

The honors of Viscount Allenby are quite extraordinary. How do British military experts compare his generalship in WWI to that of Montgomery in WWII?

Field Marshal Edmund Allenby GCB GCMB GCVO, 1st Viscount Allenby of Megiddo, was one of the more successful British generals of the First World War. He led the Egyptian Expeditionary Force (EEF)—a mixed formation of British, Egyptian, Australian, New Zealand, and Indian units, with Arab and Armenian supporters—in the occupation of Palestine and Syria in 1917 and 1918, as the Turkish Ottoman Empire collapsed.

Like Montgomery a generation later, he was seen by his troops as professional, dynamic, and inspiring, after predecessors who were thought indecisive. Both were popular for regularly visiting their troops, and one of Allenby's first moves was to relocate his headquarters from Cairo to Rafah—less comfortable, but closer to the front line.

In appearance there was no similarity. Allenby was a large man (known as "the Bull") and always impeccably turned out, while Monty famously delighted in wearing an adopted tank regiment black beret, with two badges. But Allenby shared with Monty a reputation as a sound tactician on the battlefield, careful with the lives of men—his management of the Battle of Megiddo saw hitherto unprecedented co-ordination of infantry, cavalry, and air forces. Both were demanding of staff officers, but were hard-working themselves.

Both also courted publicity. Allenby's most famous act was calculated political theatre—he entered Jerusalem on foot after the Turks had fled, to emphasize, by his humility, that he was a respecter of the traditions of a city holy to Christians, Jews, and Moslems. A photographer was on hand.

Allenby supported T.E. Lawrence in his efforts to stir an Arab Revolt, although his depiction in the 1962 film *Lawrence of Arabia*, portrayed by Jack Hawkins, unfairly cast him as duplicitous, such that his descendants issued a formal complaint against Columbia pictures. It was in fact Allenby who first suggested to US journalist Lowell Thomas that Lawrence would make a good subject for a book, which became *With Lawrence in Arabia*.

Allenby remained in the Middle East as High Commissioner for Egypt and the Sudan until 1925. His honors and awards, of which only a selection are shown in this exhibition, reflect the international nature of Britain's diplomatic power play at a pivotal time in Middle East history.

82

The story of Yeo-Thomas is quite intriguing, especially relating to the French Resistance. To what degree was he known during or after the war? Or did his duties require complete secrecy?

Wing Commander FFE Yeo-Thomas GC, MC & Bar was a British Special Operations Executive (SOE) agent during the Second World War. Code-named "The White Rabbit," he parachuted three times into France, after the second mission meeting the British Prime Minister Winston Churchill to press for greater resources to be supplied to the French Resistance. On his third mission he was betrayed and subjected to brutal torture by the Gestapo. Held in Fresnes prison, he made two failed attempts to escape and for four months was held in solitary confinement, including three weeks in a darkened cell with little food. He gave away no information, and was eventually transferred to Compiègne prison, where he twice tried to escape, and then to Buchenwald concentration camp. Here he began to organize resistance and, changing identity with a dead French prisoner, again made a brief escape. On his recapture he was sent to a French POW camp near Marienburg. He organized a mass breakout attempt from there in April 1945, finally leading 10 POWs to American lines.

In the final words of his extraordinary citation for the George Cross, he "thus turned his final mission into a success by his determined opposition to the enemy, his strenuous efforts to maintain the morale of his fellow prisoners and his brilliant escape activities. He endured brutal treatment and torture without flinching and showed the most amazing fortitude and devotion to duty throughout his service abroad, during which he was under the constant threat of death." He has been described as perhaps the bravest British secret agent of the war, so prolonged and real were his suffering, the threats to his life, and so inspiring his repeated acts of defiance.

Yeo-Thomas' set of miniature awards is shown on pages 88–89. Worn when the full-size medals would be too cumbersome, they are not officially issued but purchased privately. The medal on the extreme right—the US version of the Allied Victory Medal 1919—reflects Yeo-Thomas' earliest adventures, when in 1917 he enlisted in Paris for the US Army under a false name and age (he was just 16).

The award of Chief Commander of the Legion of Merit (page 85), given to Lord Douglas, is generally a high US honor reserved for foreign heads of state. For what act did Sholto Douglas receive this high honor?

Marshal of the Royal Air Force, Sir Sholto Douglas GCB, MC, DFC was one of the leading figures in the Royal Air Force during the Second World War. Already Deputy Chief of the Air Staff during the Battle of Britain in 1940, he succeeded Dowding as Commander in Chief (C in C) Fighter Command after the battle. In 1943 he was made C in C RAF Middle East Command, and in 1944, in the run up to D-Day, C in C Coastal Command.

In 1945 he became C in C British Air Forces of Occupation, and was the first military governor of the British Zone of Occupation. In recognition of the work he had done during the war, Douglas was knighted in January 1946 and promoted to Marshal of the RAF.

The US award of Chief Commander of the Legion of Merit, made in 1945, was "in acknowledgement and appreciation of his Second World War service and contribution to victory." Thus it did not recognize any specific act of bravery, but rather his many actions in support of US forces, which might date from as early as 1943 in North Africa, through D-Day, and to the post-war administration of Germany. The Legion of Merit has been awarded since September 8, 1939 to personnel of armed forces "friendly to the United States" in acknowledgment of "exceptionally meritorious conduct in the performance of outstanding services."

The trench art bi-plane is quite well crafted given its humble origins (page 114). How did troops in the trenches manage to fashion such fine art under adverse conditions?

"Trench Art" is a name given to a wide variety of decorative items, sometimes also functional, produced during or soon after the First World War. They were made in all the belligerent nations. Ashtrays, matchbox holders, letter knives, model tanks, and planes are typically found. Often they incorporate real bullets, brass recovered from spent charge cases, and copper from shell driving bands, although carved wooden pieces and embroideries are also seen. "Trench Art" is, however, a misleading term, as few examples were fashioned literally in the trenches—it would not have been feasible. Nor were all made by soldiers. So where did they come from?

It is probable that only the very smallest metal and wooden objects were worked by front-line soldiers, and even then mostly while in reserve lines and at rest. A greater source was workshop troops behind the lines. They had the materials, machinery, skill, and occasional spare time, and money could be made selling souvenirs to soldiers heading home. In France and Belgium, work to make souvenirs was also given to civilians displaced by the war. In all countries trench art was made "at home" during the war by those awaiting call-up; also by wounded and convalescing men, for whom handicrafts involving wood, metal, and embroidery formed part of their rehabilitation. And many discharged ex-servicemen no doubt personalized souvenirs (including those made by others) by adding inscriptions.

An often overlooked source was also the major department stores. In the immediate post-war period they offered to turn war souvenirs, such as shell fuze heads—often brought back by soldiers—into wooden-based paperweights. And if ex-soldiers had no souvenir, they could be provided. This source can be the only explanation for the widespread examples of bulkier trench art—such as dinner gongs and poker stands made from shell charge cases. These would have fit in no kitbag.

Set of 5 Medals of General Koenig
   (Order of Légion d'Honneur,
   Order of Libération, Médaille
   Militaire, and two Legion
   of Merit Medals)
Maker unknown
France, United States,
   twentieth century
Metal, textile
L: 5.3 cm; W: 7 cm
Musée de l'Armée

Badge of a Chief Commander of the Legion
   of Merit
Awarded to British Air Chief Marshal Douglas
Maker unknown
United States, 1945
Silver gilt, enamel
D: 7.4 cm
Imperial War Museum (OMD 2313)

In WWII, the French relied heavily on General Marie-Pierre Koenig. He joined General de Gaulle in London to be Chief of Staff of the First Division of the Free French Forces, and later served as Free French Delegate to Supreme Allied headquarters, under General Dwight D. Eisenhower. On page 85 are General Koenig's and British Air Chief Marshal Shalto Douglas's Legion of Merit awards. The U.S. Department of Defense issued these awards to personnel of armed forces friendly to the U.S. The medal has a five-pointed white star with 13 stars in the center of a blue disk. "United States of America" is engraved in the center on the back.

85

Victoria Cross
Awarded to William Johnstone
Hanocks & Co.
Great Britain, 1856
Copper alloy, ribbon not original
H: 3.8 cm; W: 3.5 cm
Natural History Museum of
Los Angeles County

Designs were proposed by jeweler Bailey, Banks, and Biddle, and the medal was first awarded in 1942. The overall design of the Legion of Merit was no doubt influenced by the French Légion d'honneur. The only U.S. decoration showing distinctions of rank (Chief Commander, Commander, Officer, and Legionnaire), it resembles a European award. It is also one of two decorations to be authorized as a neck decoration. The U.S. Medal of Honor is the other.

Britain's Victoria Cross is the highest military decoration of the British Order list, taking precedence over all other decorations. It is awarded for valor "in the presence of the enemy and shall then have performed some signal act of valour or devotion to their country." Introduced by Queen Victoria in 1856 for acts of valor during the Crimean War, the medal has since been awarded to nearly 1,400 individuals (in contrast to the nearly 3,500 Medal of Honor recipients in the U.S., whose military forces far exceed those of Britain). One of the first Victoria Crosses on page 86 was awarded to William

Johnstone, Royal Navy, for his military actions in 1854.

Designed in a cross pattée of bronze metal, the Victoria Cross depicts a crown surmounted by a lion, with the motto "For Valour" running beneath. The reverse reveals the date of the act, engraved within a simple circle. The cross is suspended by a ring, attached to a bar by a v-shaped bronze bar ornamented with laurel leaves, through which the ribbon passes. Etched on the back side of the bar are the recipient's name, rank, number, and unit. Originally, the ribbon for the Army and the Royal Air Force (RAF) was crimson, and the ribbon for the Navy was blue, but since 1918, the ribbon for all the armed forces has been a uniform crimson.

The Dickin Medal, created in 1943 and still awarded today, is considered to be the Victoria Cross for animals. The medal is bronze and the ribbon is composed of green, brown, and light blue stripes. The collar and lead of one Dickin

Dog Collar and Lead, decorated with Dickin
    Medal; PDSA Allied Forces Mascot Medal;
    Star Dog of Whitehaven Medal; Red Cross
    Fundraising Medal
Maker unknown
United Kingdom, c. 1940–1945
Leather, bronze, other metals
Collar: D: 14.9 cm / H with medals: 15.5 cm
Imperial War Museum (EPH 4540)

winner from 1945, Rex the dog, can be seen on page 87. Rex was officially recorded displaying "outstanding bravery in finding bomb victims trapped under fallen debris." The only American recipient from WWII was carrier pigeon G.I. Joe, honored by the Mayor of London in 1946 for saving the lives of British soldiers in Calvi Vecchia, Italy. The city was set to be bombarded by American planes at eleven o'clock on the morning of October 18, 1943, but the mission was cancelled after G.I. Joe delivered a message that the British had captured the village.

Britain's second-highest honor, the George Cross, is generally given for actions outside of realm of the distinctly military. A good example, on page 88-89, is in the group of medal miniatures, worn with evening dress, headed by the George Cross. Lieutenant Yeo-Thomas was awarded this George Cross for his work with the French Resistance, under the code name "White Rabbit" or "Shelley." Thomas was a British citizen, but lived in France for most of his life. When the war began, he joined the RAF and in 1943 was parachuted into France. After convincing

Churchill to donate arms and support, within two months he had set up a central Resistance Headquarters using disguises and ingenious tricks to avoid capture. The Gestapo finally captured him, but Thomas never gave the names of his resistance friends. After the war he was an important witness at the Nuremberg War Trials, identifying many officials associated with the Buchenwald death camp. Instituted in 1940, the George Cross consists of a plain cross with four equal arms (Greek Cross), with a circular medallion depicting St. George and the dragon,

Group of 13 Medal Miniatures
worn by Yeo-Thomas
Maker unknown
United Kingdom, c. 1950
Metal (nonspecific), textile
Average of each: L: 6 cm;
D: .3 cm; W: 2 cm;
Imperial War Museum (OMD 6854)

surrounded by the inscription, "FOR GAL-LANTRY."

Another famous George Cross recipient was the French-born Berthe Emilie Vicogne, who married an Englishman and became Mrs. Fraser. Accompanying White Rabbit on his missions with La Résistance, Mrs. Fraser arranged a hearse and hid Thomas to take him to an important rendezvous. She was one of the first post-war recipients of the American Medal of Freedom which is shown on page 89. Mrs. Fraser also received a Légion d'honneur for her work.

Medal of Freedom
Awarded to Berthe Emilie Fraser
Maker unknown
United States, c. 1945
Bronze
L: 7.5 cm; W: 3.5 cm
Imperial War Museum (OMD 4360)

Légion d'honneur
Distributed at Boulogne
Martin-Guillaume Biennais
France, 1804
Gold, enamel
D: 4.5 cm
Private Collection

Légion d'honneur of Napoléon
Martin-Guillaume Biennais
Paris, c. 1808
Gold, enamel
L: 2.4 cm; H: 3.8 cm
Ledoux Napoléon Art Collection

The Légion d'honneur is accorded to in-dividuals for their military or civil meritorious service and is the highest order accorded by France. The honor was created by Napoléon in 1802 and first awarded in 1804 on July 14TH at the Invalides. The second distribution on August 16, 1804, at the camp de Boulogne, was very symbolic. According to collector Jean-Pascal Tranié, "Napoléon had gathered over 100,000 soldiers to invade Great Britain and wanted to motivate them. One year later Napoléon redirected this army, now known as the *Grande Armée* or Great Army, to central Europe and won the famous Battle of Austerlitz on December 2, 1805." The legacy of Napoléon has been a textbook of military strategy for generations worldwide, including courses on his campaigns taught at West Point.

On page 90 (on the left) is the original model of the Légion d'honneur. It is distinctive as it features Napoléon's profile much larger as compared to three later versions in which his profile is smaller. Napoléon's medal, on page 90 (on the right) was created by his goldsmith Martin Guillaume Biennais. The design of the Légion d'honneur evolved after the first empire. By 1870, during the third republic, the head of Marianne, who was the symbol of the French Republic, was featured in the center of the decoration.

After WWII the wearing of orders, medals, and decorations of the Third Reich was forbidden in West Germany, as was any display of the Nazi emblem. The West Point Museum describes the Castle of Klessheim in Austria (as a repository of safety for a number of valuable metals and materials deemed too valuable to be left in heavily bombed Germany), uncovered by the U.S. Army. On page 91, we can see the Honor Decoration of the First Degree of the German Social Welfare Cross. Encrusted with diamonds, gold, and enamel, it was given to Madame Maria Antonesca, the wife of the Romanian dictator, the only recipient of this medal.

The military actions since the Second World War have been recognized with any number of military citations, though best known to civilians

is the Purple Heart, awarded to those wounded in action. The U.S. Medal of Honor has been awarded more than 3,400 times since the Civil War, with almost half of those accorded during that conflict alone. The Medal of Honor was awarded 464 times in World War II, and 246 were awarded during Vietnam. At the present time, this highest recognition has been the subject of some controversy because only a small number of Medals of Honor have been bestowed during the wars in Iraq and Afghanistan.

Honor Decoration of the First Degree of the
   German Social Welfare Cross
Maker unknown
Germany, c. 1940
Gold, silver, diamonds, enamel, silk ribbon bow
In Silver Casket: L: 20.3 cm; W: 15.9 cm; D: 4.4 cm
*West Point Museum Collection, United States
   Military Academy, West Point, New York*

MEMORIES

Sweetheart Brooch, 1915
Birmingham
Origin unknown, 1915
Silver
H: 3 cm; W: 1.9 cm
On loan courtesy of the Council of the National
Army Museum, London

Mementos exchanged between families and sweethearts during wartime represent a significant segment of patriotic objects. When the husband of George Patton's daughter Bee, Lt. Col. John Knight Waters, was reported missing in action after the American defeat at Kasserine Pass in Tunisia in 1943, Patton went to look for him, according to family biographer Robert Patton. "Georgie . . . who hadn't been involved in the battle, visited the site in search of Waters's remains. Finding nothing, he picked up a spent ammunition clip and sent it to Bee's sons as a memento of their father. Several weeks later he learned that Waters had been captured by the Germans." Waters survived the capture and served in the army until his retirement in 1966.

One of the earliest "memory" brooches in this collection, on page 93, dates back to the Civil War. It was created by Tiffany & Co to honor General Robert Anderson's service in defense of Fort Sumter, South Carolina, where the first shots of the Civil War were fired. A graduate of West Point, Anderson was born in Louisville, Kentucky, and though pro-slavery and a former slave-owner, he remained loyal to the Union. Against all orders, outnumbered and outgunned, Anderson and 140 men (thirteen of them musicians) defended Fort Sumter against the Confederates for four months, until finally forced to surrender and evacuate on April 13, 1861. Then a famous war hero, Anderson was immediately promoted to General. He brought the Fort Sumter flag with its thirty-three stars to New York for a rally in Union Square, then traveled with it around the North, using it as a recruiting tool. It is interesting to note that this commemorative pin has thirty-four stars. After the war, Anderson returned to Sumter and raised the fort's flag over the destroyed fort.

In 1845, when the independent republic of Texas declared it would become the twenty-eighth U.S. state, Mexico disputed the United States' claim of land north of the Rio Grande and broke off diplomatic relations with the U.S. After the Mexicans killed members of the U.S. Cavalry patrolling the disputed territory in 1846, Congress declared war. After two years of one-sided

1861 Fort Sumter Decoration
Memory broach belonging to the Anderson Family
Tiffany & Co.
New York City, c. 1861
Gold medallion, enamel, braided silk insert
W: 3.8 cm; H: 4.4 cm
West Point Museum Collection, United States Military Academy, West Point, New York

Medal of the Military Order of the Dragon
Maker unknown
Origin unknown, c. 1905
Blackened or painted bronze with gilt dragon,
 silk ribbon
Pendant: D: 4.8 cm / Ribbon: W: 3.8 cm
West Point Museum Collection, United States
 Military Academy, West Point, New York

battles, with many of its major cities occupied and facing insurmountable opposition, Mexico was forced to sign the Treaty of Guadalupe Hidalgo, ceding to the U.S. undisputed control of Texas, as well as the territory comprising the states of California, Nevada, Utah, and parts of New Mexico, Colorado, Wyoming, and Arizona, and establishing the Rio Grande as the border between the two countries. In return, the U.S. gave Mexico approximately $18 million (less than half of what the U.S. offered to Mexico before the War) and assumed $3 million of Mexican debts. Internal disagreements among Americans over the decision to take part in this conflict helped pave the way for the Civil War; U.S. military leaders who fought as officers during the Mexican War included Stonewall Jackson, Ulysses S. Grant, Robert E. Lee, and Jefferson Davis. To

commemorate the fiftieth anniversary of the Mexican-American War (1846-1848), Tiffany minted the medal on page 29 for the Aztec Club, formed in 1847 to honor heroic acts of officers.

Like the Aztec Club, the Military Order of the Dragon was formed to perpetuate the memory of those American soldiers who served in the Boxer Rebellion in China. At the beginning of the twentieth century, a secret Chinese society known as the Righteous Harmonious Fists, referred to by Westerners as "boxers" because of their martial arts, endeavored to have "foreign devils" (imperialists) expelled from China. Their wrath was provoked by expanding Western commercial enclaves, accompanied by Christian missionaries. Beginning in the spring of 1900, 3,400 American Navy seamen and officers arrived in China on the *Oregon* and

Sweetheart Brooch, the Buffs
  (Royal East Kent Regiment)
Maker unknown
Origin unknown, c. 1942
Brass, mother of pearl, enamel
D: 2.9 cm
On loan courtesy of the
  Council of the National
  Army Museum, London

the *Newark* as part of an eight-nation alliance including Russia, Britain, Germany, Japan, Italy, France, and Austria-Hungary. These forces consisted of highly trained marines who were quickly able to quell the rebellion. For their service in quelling the rebellion, the Americans were awarded the medal on page 94, which was cast in bronze with a gold overlay resembling a dragon.

As far back as Mesopotamia, people carried special amulets which they believed possessed magical powers to bring luck or ward off evil. During World War I and through World War II, soldiers helped to create or bought charms for sweethearts: their wives, mothers, sisters, or girlfriends. Europeans, for the most part, created small hand-made jeweled representations of their regiments or units, unlike the Americans who mass-produced charms. Also unlike France,

Sweetheart Brooch in the shape of
  a light infantry bugle
Maker unknown
Origin unknown, c. 1941
Silver, enamel
H: 3 cm; W: 2.8 cm
On loan courtesy of the Council of the
  National Army Museum, London

Sweetheart Brooch, decorated with the divisional
  sign of 30 Corps.
Maker unknown
Origin unknown, c. 1942
Brass, enamel
D: 4 cm
*On loan courtesy of the Council of the National
  Army Museum, London*

bought in 1915 by Lt. David Edward Westwater's sister, Margaret, was dedicated to her brother for his service with the 21 Field Squadron Royal Engineers. Lt. Westwater enlisted in 1938 and was tragically killed in action in March 1943, south of Mareth, Tunisia, at the age of 26. The silver brooch, hallmarked Birmingham, depicts the regimental badges of the Royal Engineers with the royal cipher representing King George V adorning the center of the piece.

The sweetheart brooch given by Private Cyril Harry Goodwin to his sister, Mrs. Ethel Goodwin Brown, on page 95 has a brass regimental badge with an enameled scroll surrounding a disc made from mother-of-pearl. Goodwin had joined the Queen's Royal Regiment (West Surrey), which is England's oldest infantry regiment, formed in 1661 under King Charles II.

Also on page 95 is a sweetheart brooch made in the shape of a light infantry bugle from 1941. The brooch is crafted in silver and blue enamel with cord straps and tassels forming a decorative loop above an inscription on the scroll below.

where gold legally needed to be 18-karat, 14-karat gold was often the chosen material in the U.S.

More European regimental badges fashioned from precious jewelry are shown on pages 92 and 95. According to the National Army Museum, the sweetheart brooch on page 92, originally

This sweetheart brooch belonged to the mother of Michael Handford. In 1941, Handford joined the Oxford and Buckinghamshire Light Infantry and two years later was commissioned into the Royal Army Service Corps.

The Buffs Regimental Museum Collection was donated in its entirety to the National Army Museum in 2000, including the sweetheart brooch on page 96. It is associated with Captain T.W. Manning who served in a Western Desert formation that distinguished itself in 1942 at El Alamein. The historic battle of El Alamein in October 1942 turned the tide in the African campaign. According to Winston Churchill, "Before Alamein we never had a victory. After Alamein we never had a defeat." The brooch is made in brass and enameled in black and white and decorated with the divisional sign of 30 Corps.

On page 97 is a handmade British sweetheart brooch box from WWII. The box was made by Major CRG Barrington for his wife, Dr. Kathleen Barrington, who was evacuated to Canada and subsequently employed as a psychi-

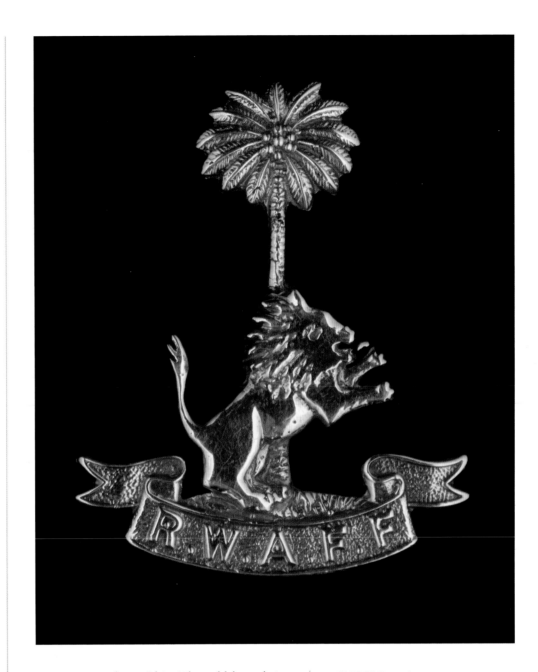

atrist in Hamilton, Ohio. The gold brooch is embossed with the initials "RWAFF" (Royal West African Frontier Force) and decorated with a roaring lion superimposed over a palm tree trunk. The brooch box is adorned with an intertwined KMB monogram.

RWAFF Brooch
Major CRG Barrington
Sierra Leone, Freetown, 1942–1943
Gold
H: 7 cm; W: 5.7 cm
Imperial War Museum (INS 773)

PHILIP ATTWOOD

Philip Attwood is Keeper of Coins and Medals at the British Museum. He has written widely on medals and badges. For many years he has edited *The Medal*, the international journal of the British Art Medal Society. He is currently the Society's president and the UK delegate to the Fédération Internationale de la Médaille d'Art (FIDEM).

The George Washington Peace Medal (page 119) is quite unusual, especially coming from a British collection. What is the story behind it?

Ever since the British Museum was founded in 1753, its collection has been enlarged by both donations and purchases. The most important early addition in terms of medals was the gift of the large collection put together by George III, which was presented to the Museum by his son George IV in 1823. Included in this huge body of material was an intriguing engraved silver Indian peace medal from the United States of about 1776. It has a portrait of George Washington on one side and on the other a representation of a Native American figure seated by a column towards which thirteen hands reach out. The column evokes the ancient Roman Republic and the virtues associated with it; the hands represent the thirteen colonies that had rebelled against British rule. The medal still has the loop with which it could be attached to clothing and worn.

How this piece came into the royal collection is unknown, although historical records suggest a possible route. In 1777 the U.S. government gave silver medals to representatives of the Micmac and Maliseet Indians, with whom it had formed an alliance the previous year. In September 1778 some of the tribal chiefs were persuaded to join with the British, and it is recorded that they then handed over the gifts they had received from the Americans. In an article published in 1985, Harald Prins suggested that this medal was perhaps one of those gifts and that the British commander then presented it to his king as a symbol of this minor diplomatic success—and that it was in this way that it eventually found its way into the British Museum. The suggestion seems plausible.

One of the aspects of this medal that makes it especially interesting is that the designs on its two sides were produced by hand-engraving. This contrasts with most medals presented to Native Americans by both Britain and the United States, which were made by the striking process (the process by which coins are made). An example of a struck medal of this sort is provided by another object in the British Museum's collection, which is always of great interest to American visitors to the Museum. It is a rare example of the largest of three sizes of medals, and bears a portrait of Jefferson and the date 1801. These were given out on the Lewis and Clark expedition of 1804 to 1806, with the largest size going only to the most important Indian chiefs. But the excitement of the Washington medal lies

98

in its individual workmanship. Each medal of this engraved type (and very few are known) was hand-made. Perhaps inevitably, the name of Paul Revere has been associated with them.

The Boer War, where Churchill first distinguished himself, was apparently marked by numerous commemorative badges. What is the significance of those displayed here (pages 43 and 99)?

The Boer War of 1899–1902 coincided with an extraordinary upsurge of imperialist fervor in Britain, to which the badges exhibited here are witness. "England expects every man to do his duty" paraphrases the famous signal sent by Nelson to his men at the beginning of the Battle of Trafalgar in 1805. This decisive victory against Napoléonic France and Nelson's death during the battle consolidated the phrase as a patriotic cry in the popular imagination. "Let the hunters 'ware who flout him when he calls his whelps about him" is taken from an imperialist poem of 1899, *The Lion's Whelps*, by the Australian poet George Essex Evans. The lion in question is Britain and the whelps are the country's colonies and dominions, some named on the badge, that have answered the call to fight. Iron-ically, despite their patriotic messages, these two badges have paper inserts in their backs revealing that they were made by the Whitehead & Hoag Company, Newark, New Jersey, and must therefore have been imported into Britain. This type of badge

Boer War Badge
 —"Let the hunters . . ."
Whitehead & Hoag
Newark, c. 1900
Base metal, celluloid, paper
D without pin: 2.2 cm
The British Museum

was quite new at this time. It was developed in the United States in the 1890s, with Whitehead & Hoag taking out a series of patents for its novel and ingenious method of manufacture, which was first used for making trouser buttons.

Other badges circulating in Britain at this time showed the generals and commanders of the British forces, while others celebrated the triumphant return of the soldiers. The two examples displayed here on page 100 welcome back the City of London Imperial Volunteers, or CIVs; the shield placed prominently on them is that of the City of London. The CIVs were part of a voluntary force formed in

December 1899 after Britain had suffered an early setback in the war. Having distinguished themselves in battle, they returned to London on October 29, 1900 for a formal entry into the city, a thanksgiving service at St Paul's cathedral, a reception at the Guildhall, and a banquet. However, the huge and often unruly crowds, many of whom would have worn badges like these, proved too much for the forces of law and order, and chaotic scenes ensued. The welcoming ceremony at the entrance to the city had to be abandoned and the soldiers were scarcely able to maintain their marching formation. As *The Times* reported the following day, "it was

clear that someone had blundered." The volunteers arrived at St Paul's only after "one of the most trying marches accomplished even by a body which has won such praise for its marching powers."

The Great War brought together numerous allies. What is the significance of the commemorative flags pictured on page 102?

Whereas the Boer War badges focused on Britain, its history and empire, these badges highlight the nature of the First World War as a conflict between two opposing alliances of sovereign states. The colorful butterfly has wings formed from the flags of Belgium, Japan, France, and Britain, whilst its body carries the Imperial Russian ensign. On the other badge the same flags reappear as five playing cards held in a hand, as if to indicate that this is a winning combination. The inclusion of these five nations, the major allies against Germany and Austria-Hungary at the outbreak of the war, suggests that these badges belong to 1914 or early 1915. Italy, which was to join the war on the allied side in April 1915, is not represented, and the advent of the United States into the war in 1917 and the Russian Revolution of the same year would have rendered the badges obsolete. The popular enthusiasm for the war, especially strong in Britain in the War's first months is reflected in these

World War II Badge—"V" with Flags
Maker unknown
United Kingdom, 1945
Base metal, paper
W: 3.1 cm
The British Museum

commitment to duty. Gas masks were issued to the entire population at the beginning of the war and anyone found without one could be fined, but in the end there were no gas attacks—and so the humor of Vincze's medal did not sour.

In the same category we see a flag pin on page 109 derived from banners displayed by American mothers of soldiers serving in both World Wars. What is the significance of this particular blue star design?

The patriotic nature of this American badge is made clear by its colors: red, white, and blue. The stars representing two "boys in uniform" also have an obvious association with the United States. This sort of badge was worn by mothers of soldiers serving in the First World War. It was made using the same technique as those exported to Britain during the Boer War, a technique that is still in use today. The enduring appeal of this manufacturing method results from its simplicity, which renders it an economical way of transmitting a message. More or less anyone can afford such an item—an important consideration during times of war when appeals to patriotism are that much more vital.

highly decorative personal adornments.

A similar motif appears in a badge of the Second World War also exhibited here on page 101. The British flag is accompanied by those of France, the Soviet Union, the United States and the Republic of China, the major allies in the war after 1941. The central V for Victory and inscription, "Peace & Freedom," show that the badge was made for the victory celebrations of 1945.

In addition to elaborate designs and materials, recognition was also evident for civilians on the home front. Tell us about the air raid protection medal on page 103.

In this humorous silver medal the artist Paul Vincze shows Cupid, the winged god of love, as a chubby child carrying his customary bow, arrow, and quiver in the traditional manner. But Vincze has added other elements that show that this particular Cupid is a responsible deity who has done his patriotic duty and volunteered as an Air Raid Protection warden. ARP wardens performed a wide range of duties in Britain during the Second World War, including ensuring that no lights could be seen at night and that members of the public had their gas masks with them. This Cupid wears the ARP warden's protective metal helmet and dutifully carries his gas mask. His vigilant pose indicates his

World War I Badge—Butterfly
Maker unknown
United Kingdom, c. 1914
Silver, colored enamel
W: 3.4 cm
The British Museum

World War I Badge—Cards
Maker unknown
United Kingdom, c. 1914
Base metal, enamel
W: 2.6 cm
The British Museum

Rings were often made to celebrate patriotism during the two wars. On page 103 is an iron finger ring engraved with "gold gab ich für Eisen 1914 OSK." The inscription "gold for iron" recalls the century-old German tradition of donating jewelry to make armaments. Adele Frankl, who lived in Innsbruck, gave all her gold jewelry away in 1914 and received this ring of iron in return as a reward for doing her patriotic duty.

The second finger ring on page 103 was fashioned in gold with red, white, and blue stones for Evelyn Pearl by her fiancé Yves Jaulmes. He had it made in Paris, but the jeweler refused to imprint his trademark for fear of identification because the Schutzstaffel (SS) was vigilant for any signs or symbols of resistance.

A charm designed by Cartier France, on page 104, takes the shape of an airplane. Originally stamped with a date 1916, it was later modified to read "1918," the year marking the end of WWI. The other Cartier charm commemorating the end of that war, on page 104, has the

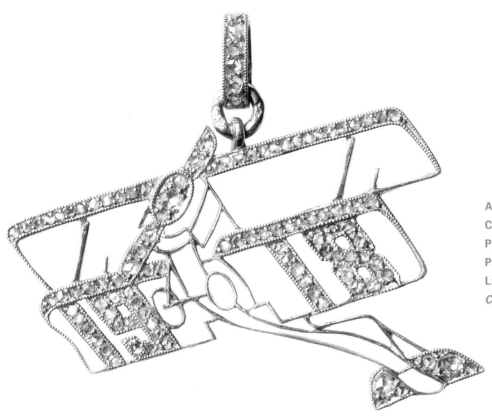

Airplane Charm
Cartier
Paris, 1916
Platinum, diamonds
L: 1 cm; W: 2.8 cm
Cartier Collection

1918 Charm
Cartier
Paris, 1917
Platinum, diamonds
W: 1.65 cm; H: 1.53 cm
Cartier Collection

Locket Medallion with Helmet
Joseph Chaumet
Paris, c. 1917
Gold, blue steel, diamonds
D: 2.4 cm; H: 3 cm
Collection Chaumet Paris

name of the sweetheart engraved on the back—Georgette Gaston, March 21, 1918.

The venerable jewelry firm Chaumet, which created pieces for Napoléon I, was likewise inspired to design commemorative jewels after the Great War. On page 104 is a gold, steel, and diamond locket representing a helmet. The blue steel background encloses a miniature photograph of a young man, and might have also enclosed a lock of hair. Another Chaumet patriotic jewel is the Red Cross medallion on page 105, made in platinum and decorated with rubies, diamonds, and sapphires. It was a gift from Joseph Chaumet to his daughter who, during WWI, worked as a nurse for the Red Cross. The medallion—featuring the three colors of the French flag—can be worn as a pendant or on a charm bracelet.

Charms and charm bracelets sometimes evoke bittersweet memories. During WWII, Boucheron created the 18-karat gold charm bracelet with eight charms on page 106, called "The Restriction Train." It symbolizes the main

restricted items of wartime: sugar, wine, oil, and coffee, led by an engine and three railway cars. Hermès memorialized the restrictions of war in the silver objects seen on page 106. The first is

Red Cross Medallion
Joseph Chaumet
Paris, 1917
Platinum, diamonds, rubies, sapphires
D: 2.4 cm; H: 3 cm
Collection Chaumet Paris

Bracelet "Le train des restrictions" ("Restriction Train")
Boucheron
France, 1942
Gold
L: 18 cm
Boucheron

Boîte à mégots ("Cigarette Butts Box")
Hermès
France, 1940
Silver plated brass
L: 4 cm; W: 4 cm; H: 1.5 cm
Collections du Conservatoire des Créations Hermès

Boîte à sucre ("Sugar Box")
Hermès
France, 1940
Silver plated brass
L: 5 cm; W: 4 cm; H: 1.3 cm
Collections du Conservatoire des Créations Hermès

Boîte à sucre (Sugar Box)
Maker unknown
France, 1918
Silver
L: 7 cm; W: 4.7 cm; H: 1.3 cm
Collection Emile Hermès

Touch Wood Lighter
Alfred Dunhill
Great Britain, 1941
Silver plate, mahogany
L: 6 cm; W: 4 cm
Alfred Dunhill Museum and Archive

a silver box for cigarette butts; the second is a silver box for sugar. During the war, civilians carried sugar with them to dinner parties and restaurants because this resource was so scarce. Emile Hermès possesses another sugar box, although not made by Hermès, on page 107, which not only held sugar but also carries the inscription "*mon sucre,*" or "my sugar." Unlike the previous objects, this sugar box was actually made during the First World War.

Because luck so often played a role in

whether a soldier lived or died, Alfred Dunhill created "Touch Wood" lighters during WWII, using timber salvaged from the Dunhill store ruined during The Blitz (see page 107). Alfred Henry Dunhill, the son of the founder, Alfred Dunhill, is pictured outside the site of the devastation welcoming customers in April 1941.

Alfred Henry Dunhill
Great Britain, 1941
Alfred Dunhill Museum and Archive

Charm Bracelet
Tiffany & Co.
United States, c. 1944
14k gold
L: 18 cm; W: 2.5 cm
Tiffany & Co. Archives

Bangle
Tiffany & Co.
United States, 1943–1945
Sterling silver, gold, ruby,
  diamond, sapphire
L: 1.9 cm; W: 6.35 cm D: 6.3 cm
Tiffany & Co. Archives

During both wars, Tiffany was a favorite American purveyor of patriotic jewelry, especially with their unique charm bracelets. The Tiffany bracelet on page 108 has six charms: an American eagle and "U.S.A." framed within a circle, the Statue of Liberty, a replica of the Navy's Catalina PBY-5A, a hand showing victory, a St. Christopher's medal used for protection on journeys (St. Christopher is revered among mariners), and an anchor with the initials for the U.S. Navy (encircled in a medallion). Most likely this bracelet was bought for the sweetheart of a naval pilot.

As both gold and silver were in short supply, Tiffany, along with jewelry industry representatives and the photo-engravers association, lobbied Washington to release a small stock of domestically produced silver. When the government relented, Tiffany was able to produce a small number of silver bangles promoting the memory of loved ones who had served in the military. The sterling silver Tiffany bangle on page 108 is complete with a ruby, a diamond, and a sapphire star resembling the star used to denote sons and daughters serving in the war. Such stars were displayed in WWI and throughout WWII on the War Mother's flag, which families draped in windows of their homes. Beneath the American flag is the service flag or blue star flag, which was flown on Veterans Day; if a child was in the service, a blue star was shown in the middle of the white background, but if the son or daughter had been killed, the blue star was replaced by a gold one. On page 109 are two poignant examples of this image: the first is a plastic and metal badge from WWI, with two blue stars indicating two children serving in the war; the other is an exquisitely created pin from WWII, adorned with diamonds and sapphires.

World War I Badge—2 Stars
Maker unknown
United States, c. 1942
Base metal, celluloid, paper
D without pin: 2.3 cm
The British Museum

Service Flag Badge
Maker unknown
United States, c. 1940s
White gold, diamonds, rubies, sapphire
H: 1 cm; W: 1.6 cm
Victoria and Albert Museum, London, given by
   the American Friends of the V&A through the
   generosity of Patricia V. Goldstein

Yvonne Markowitz

Yvonne J. Markowitz is the Rita J. Kaplan and Susan B. Kaplan Curator of Jewelry in the David and Roberta Logie Department of Textile and Fashion Arts, Museum of Fine Arts, Boston. The first curatorship of its kind in America, Ms. Markowitz oversees the museum's exceptional collection of jewelry.

What is the difference between "trench art" ornaments and "sweetheart" jewelry?

The popular view is that "trench art" jewelry refers to adornments made by soldiers stationed in France during WWI. However, the subject is broader and has come to include soldier art from both earlier and later wars as well as ornaments made by prisoners of war, convalescing soldiers, and enterprising civilians in and around conflict areas. The jewelry has a folk-art quality and is typically crafted from non-precious materials, such as spent shell casings, shrapnel, fuse caps, and airship parts—all products of the mechanization of war that were found in abundance on the battlefield. Coins were also worked as a raw material and could be melted down and cast into adornments. Although most of the jewelry was made for loved ones back home, some ornaments were crafted as personal mementos of the war and worn by those in uniform. Many of these items bear inscriptions that include names, dates, and battlefields. The most common forms of jewelry made were finger rings and brooches.

"Sweetheart" jewelry first appeared during WWI and later became highly fashionable during the Second World War when mobilization of the civilian sector was seen as a vital component of the war effort. The jewelry, which was worn by the sweethearts, sisters, wives, and mothers of those serving in the armed forces, gave testimony to their patriotism and sacrifice. Unlike "trench art" ornaments, which were largely hand-fabricated, a good deal of "sweetheart" jewelry was mass-produced commercially and sold not only in military PXs (Post Exchanges) but in small shops, department stores, and mail-order houses on the home front. All forms of jewelry were made in this genre with brooches, bracelets, and charms dominating. Many of the ornaments spell out a branch of military service (US Army, US Navy, and USMC) while others display military emblems associated with the different services. Additionally, enameled pins with one or more five-pointed stars ("in-service stars") were worn to indicate the number of family members on active duty. "V" for Victory brooches, "Remember Pearl Harbor" adornments, and patriotic lockets incorporating photos of servicemen were also popular. As for the materials used, most items were made of base metal, silver/gold plate, silver, wood, aluminum, shell, mother-of-pearl, or plastic. However, several high-style firms, such as Tiffany & Co., Trabert, Hoeffer-Mauboussin, Inc., and J.E. Caldwell of Philadelphia, made similar adornments using precious materials.

How were soldiers capable of making "trench art" jewelry without tools and machines?

During WWI, soldiers in many parts of the Western Front experienced relatively quiet intervals with little activity. To pass the time, battlefield detritus would be collected and worked with the simplest of tools, including knives, files, and screwdrivers. Other tools, such as gravers, were constructed from nails and scrap metal, while more sophisticated devices would sometimes be acquired by soldiers on leave. Some soldiers, especially those with an engineering or metals background, had access to repair and tool maintenance shops where they could use professional equipment for cutting, sanding, drilling, and metal spinning.

The adornments created by soldiers demonstrate a wide range of skills, with the most sophisticated objects fabricated by those trained in the applied arts. However, skills were shared and many soldiers returned home with basic metalworking knowledge. The decorative techniques most frequently employed in fabricating jewelry were hammering, chasing, engraving, and *repoussé* or appliqué work. When metal needed to be annealed (heated) to shape or decorate an ornament, it was placed in a wood fire, worked, and then cooled in the ashes.

Are there any significant differences between the sweetheart jewelry of various nations?

While the jewelry forms remain relatively constant (e.g., rings, bracelets, brooches, and neck ornaments), the motifs employed vary from country to country. For example, a common British Royal Air Force brooch features the letters RAF flanked by outstretched wings, whereas a comparable Army Air Force pin in the United States depicts wings with a central propeller blade. However, some motifs were popular in more than one country. An example is the "V" for Victory brooch based on Winston Churchill's use of a "v" sign as a symbol of hope and call to action. It inspired not only the British but also the Americans, French, and Dutch. Another ornament with widespread appeal was the bracelet/ brooch with miniature flags and emblems of the Allied Powers—a brief show of solidarity among several nations, some of whom would later become Cold War adversaries.

Other adornments identified a soldier's theater of operation, often incorporating coins from a variety of countries within a region. For example, a sterling silver charm bracelet provides a glimpse into the activities of a one U.S. soldier. His image, along with that of his wife or sweetheart, appears in the form of a miniature photograph mounted inside a hinged photo album. The bracelet also incorporates military charms that designate the serviceman as having served overseas. They include a pair of field glasses, a Pacific anti-aircraft artillery gun, crossed rifles, a U.S. jeep with star, a tank, a heart with U.S. Army insignia, a Lockheed P 38 long-range fighter plane, and a helmet. Interspersed throughout are coins of U.S. allies (England, Canada, and Australia) as well as a 1944 Philippine ten-centavo piece, suggesting that the soldier served in the Pacific (see page 111).

Variations of "sweetheart" jewelry include

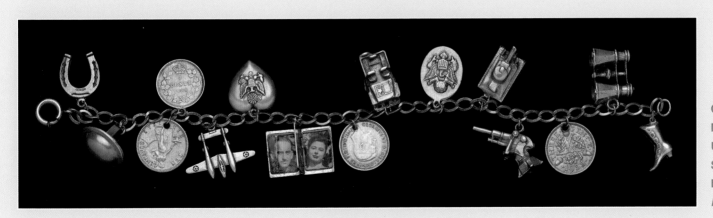

Charm Bracelet
Maker unknown
United States, 1944
Silver
L: 21 cm; L charms: 2.5 cm each
Private Collection

ornaments worn by those on the home front involved in wartime industries and activities. The most popular was the "E" for Excellence pin awarded for outstanding effort on the job. The pins, stamped with the words, "Army-Navy Production Award" on reverse, were issued on a card with the following signed message by Frank Delano Roosevelt: "An Army-Navy Production Award emblem is a symbol of service in the greatest force in the world today—a united and free army of American workers." The "E" pin worn by Norman Rockwell's Rosie the Riveter would have been awarded for having driven no fewer than 3,345 rivets in six hours.

Other home-front ornaments reflect the important role of volunteers in USO Clubs, first-aid courses, water safety classes, and air-raid monitoring. Each organization had its identifying pin or badge—this particular one (see page 112) belonged to Anna Freed, a school teacher in New York who participated in weekly bandage-rolling sessions.

What are the most unusual examples of "sweetheart" jewelry?

One of the most interesting examples of a war-related ornament is the "caged bird" brooch of gold and precious stones made by Cartier as a symbol of occupied France after the Nazi invasion of Paris on June 14, 1940. The jewel was a metaphoric protest of the occupation and several versions were made. When Hitler's eagle was finally removed from the city in 1944, the firm celebrated by creating the "freed bird" brooch depicting a jubilant, singing bird emerging from its cage (see page 113). The beautifully designed bird, fashioned by Cartier in coral, 18-karat gold and platinum, has wings made of lapis lazuli. Its head is decorated with rose-cut diamonds and a sapphire cabochon eye. Cartier, USA also made patriotic brooches, including a star-shaped flag brooch with a central spinel, a gemstone that is red in color, that was illustrated in *Vogue* (December 1, 1940).

Some of the most whimsical "sweetheart" ornaments were made of plastic. One example is a Bakelite representation of Kilroy ("Kilroy Was Here")—a reference to the graffiti and cartoon image that came to represent America's presence throughout the world during the Second World War. Other examples include an articulated plastic sailor with red, white, and blue rhinestone highlights and a clear Lucite heart with an emblazoned army emblem.

Can you identify "sweetheart" or "trench art" jewelry from the twenty-first century?

It's difficult to tell at this point. Both WWI and WWII were global struggles involving millions of combatants and civilians—the ubiquity of "sweetheart" jewelry and ornaments related to home front activity gives testimony to this fact. Contemporary warfare is more compartmentalized with fewer individuals directly affected—hence, fewer "sweethearts" waiting for their loved ones to return home and a diminished demand for commercially-made ornaments. As for "trench art" ornaments, the realities of the modern battlefield are not conducive to the widespread crafting of mementoes, although the urge to create something lasting and meaningful, even under dire circumstances, is a universal, human endeavor.

"E" for Excellence Pin
"American Women's Voluntary Services" pin
Maker unknown
United States, 1942–1945
White metal, enamel
"E"—H: 1.1 cm; W: 2.5 cm
"American Women's"—H: 2.9 cm; W: 1.9 cm
Private Collection

"'Trench art' refers to objects made by soldiers in the midst of combat, and it originated during the early years of WWI, when [it] was made on a scale never seen before or since," said Fullbright scholar and collector Jane A. Kimball. During the Great War, thousands of soldiers were confined in rough and remote trenches which stretched from the North Sea to the Northern border of Switzerland. They had no access to the tools and materials necessary to make fine jewelry, and therefore improvised using their battlefield knives and metal from used cartridges to produce rough but sometimes fine objects as mementos for loved ones at home.

Oiseau libéré Brooch
Cartier
Paris, 1944
Gold, platinum, diamonds, sapphire, lapis lazuli, coral
W: 2.41 cm; H: 3.72 cm
Cartier Collection

Model Bi-Plane
Maker unknown
France, 1917
Brass, copper, steel
L: 13 cm; W: 17.5 cm; H: 4.8 cm
Imperial War Museum (EPH 8110)

"Few pieces of 'trench art' were actually made in the trenches, but images of French warfare were firmly planted. . . . It is used today to describe many types of hand-crafted war souvenirs." The Battle of Verdun is often referred to by historians as "France's Stalingrad." That moment is also recalled by the lyrical model aircraft on page 114, inscribed on its upper wing with the words "Souvenir of the Verdun Campaign 1914–1917." The plane was made from brass, copper, and steel. It was the property of Private F.H. Warren who served in the Royal Army Medical Corps (RAMC) during WWI.

One of the most refined examples of trench

art is the Funeral Urn-Shaped Box on page 115 made in the memory of Jules Noël by Hermès's silversmith, Jacques Pouthier. Pouthier was taken prisoner during WWII. While in captivity he created this memorial to his comrade from drawings by Max Ingrand. The pewter box is engraved in copper and the letters were made from the bases of light bulbs. The four sides read: "Glory to the Stadium," "1903–1940," "In Honor of the Flag," and "Jules Noël." Noël, who was a French Olympic discus thrower, served in the 21ST battalion from the 43RD infantry and was killed during the French Campaign in 1940. Pouthier was able to create the pewter soldering by obtaining resin from the pinecones from which soldier beds were made. He derived a source of heat by burning a wick in fat, then blowing through a torch made from cans. In its simplicity, this glorious funeral urn makes us appreciate what soldiers in combat can achieve under the most primitive conditions.

After WWII, the bicentennial of the U.S. as well as the Cold War continued to inspire

Coupe en forme d'urne funéraire exécutée à la mémoire de Jules Noël (Cup in the shape of a Funeral Urn created in memory of Jules Noël)
Jacques Pouthier, after a design of Max Ingrand
Oflag IV-D (prisoner camp), Germany, 1942
Pewter, copper, iron, tin
L: 15 cm; W: 12 cm
Collection Emile Hermès

national images, evoking patriotism, and supporting the ethos of democracy and communism respectively (though the latter with much more austerity, to reflect their proletariat values). One extraordinary example is the Eagle Brooch on page 116. It was designed and made in 1976 in honor of America's bicentennial. It consists of

diamonds, rubies, sapphires, gold, and platinum.

Flags remain a favorite image of U.S. jewelers for commemorating conflicts into the twenty-first century, often viewed on the lapels of blazers all over the United States, including the President's (flag pins even became an election issue in 2008), as a sign of post-9/11 patriotism.

"American Flag" Brooch
Tiffany & Co.
United States, 1900–1910
Platinum, gold, rubies, sapphires, diamonds
L: 8.3 cm; W: 9.5 cm
Tiffany & Co. Archives

The flag brooch on page 117 is a beautiful example of the genre. It displays the first official American flag, the design of which was established on June 14, 1777 by the Continental Congress who resolved in the Flag Act "that the flag of the United States be made of thirteen stripes, alternate red and white; that the Union be thirteen stars, white in a blue field, representing a new Constellation" (referring to the number of original colonies that became the first states). The brooch was specially commissioned in 1900, but numerous flag brooches appear in Tiffany catalogues from 1889–1912 and remain popular contemporary images.

PEACE

Peace never evokes the passions of war, but the two are often related in the words of warriors. In George Washington's first message to Congress in 1790, he is famously quoted as warning that "to be prepared for war is one of the most effective means of preserving peace." And as we follow the story of the Patton family's military saga, George Patton remarked, "I dare say that for every man remembered for acts of peace, there are fifteen made immortal by war."

It is custom in Europe to bestow medals upon important visitors as a sign of respect when negotiating treaties. This practice was carried on in the colonies by George Washington and his new administration. The founding fathers wanted to assure the Native Americans that the newly-formed states wanted peace. In fact, early American presidents were competing with the British, the French, and the Spanish, who were already currying favor with the natives by bestowing medals in order to secure and control their trading relationships. Even after the Revolutionary War, colonial rivalries did not cease since the European powers occupied vast terri-

tories from Ohio to California. In competition for Indian commerce, the French were especially generous, not only with medals but also with gifts of all kinds, which accounted for their favor over the British. The difference in attitude can perhaps be attributed to the impetus of British immigration being an escape from problems of the old world, while France was motivated more by mercantile opportunism.

The earliest U.S. Indian Peace medal, on page 119, belongs to the British Museum. It pictures George Washington on one side, with a Native American seated at the base of a column, facing thirteen hands of the colonies on the other. It was engraved between July 1776 and June 1777. On July 4, 1776, the Congress of the United States—representing the thirteen British North American colonies that would become the first

of the United States: Pennsylvania, New Jersey, Delaware, New York, North Carolina, South Carolina, Virginia, Connecticut, Rhode Island, New Hampshire, Massachusetts, Maryland, and Georgia—declared its independence from Great

George Washington Peace Medal
Maker unknown
United States, c. 1776
Silver
D: 5.7 cm
The British Museum

Britain. Naturally, the number thirteen became highly symbolic. On the back side of the medal, the Tree of Liberty with the revolting colonies is represented by the thirteen hands.

What makes this first Peace medal exceptional is its authorship and provenance; it was believed to have been engraved by Paul Revere, America's most famous colonial silversmith. Revere's midnight ride to warn patriots in Boston of British troop movements was immortalized forty years after his death by Henry Wadsworth Longfellow's "Paul Revere's Ride": "Listen my children and you shall hear of the midnight ride of Paul Revere, on the eighteenth of April in seventy-five; hardly a man is now alive who remembers that famous day and year. . . ." The legend has made Revere into a folk hero, and his name synonymous with revolutionary patriotism. According to silver expert, James McConnaughy of Shrubsole, "The price of a Paul Revere piece of silver might be ten times the price of a similar piece by another American silversmith of the period." Pieces of his silver are rare and could fetch over $500,000. The provenance of this medal is equally unique. According to documents, King George III acquired this medal as a war trophy from his head of Indian Affairs in Canada, whose natives were rewarded for changing allegiance from the Americans to the Crown.

Some dozen years later, Indian Peace medals from the early presidents were produced by the U.S. government rather than by private craftsmen. The earliest of these, on page 120, dates to 1789, at the time of George Washington's inauguration. The front of the hand-engraved, medium-sized medal depicts a Native American, wearing his headdress and draped in a blanket. His right hand has dropped the tomahawk, and his left is accepting a peace pipe from a figure signifying the United States. In the foreground is a shield and spear, but a plow appears in the background, signifying the coming modernity that will dramatically alter the natives' way of life. The right-hand figure is most likely Minerva, the Roman goddess of wisdom. Examples of this style are extremely rare because the Washington

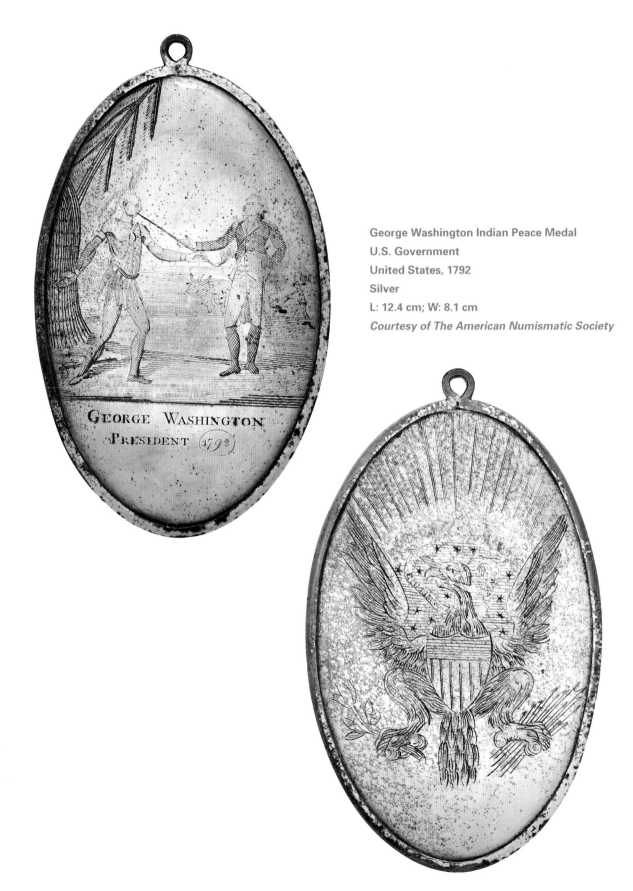

George Washington Indian Peace Medal
U.S. Government
United States, 1792
Silver
L: 12.4 cm; W: 8.1 cm
Courtesy of The American Numismatic Society

Thomas Jefferson Indian Peace Medal
U.S. Government
United States, 1801
Silver
D: 10.3 cm
Courtesy of The American Numismatic Society

administration soon exchanged the female personification with a portrait of the President himself. On the back of this medal is a powerfully drawn heraldic eagle with a thirteen-striped shield on its front. The right claw holds an olive branch and the left holds thirteen arrows.

On page 121 is an example of the new peace medals produced during the Washington administration. Unlike the first medal, which places the words "G. Washington, President" at the top, this small peace medal discreetly places the words "George Washington President" at the bottom with the date 1792 stylized by an elongation of the number 9. For this smaller medal, the Native

American is realistically dressed with only four feathers on his head (two up and two down). The larger version showed five feathers to signify the importance of the medal's receiver. The Native American is wearing a peace medal and has dropped his tomahawk to the ground. Washington wears his general's uniform and stands with a hand on his sword. The other hand reaches out for the peace pipe the Indian is smoking. In the background is a house with a man and his oxen plowing the ground—again symbolizing the arrival of modern farming methods, trade, and a joint cultivation of a shared land. On the back is the official seal of the United States. The new nation's motto, *E Pluribus Unum* (Latin for "Out of Many, One"), can be read on a ribbon carried in the eagle's beak. While never officially enacted, "*E Pluribus Unum*" was the unofficial U.S. motto until it was replaced, in 1956, by "In God We Trust." Medals at this time did not have spaces for ribbons or

attachments, so natives would pierce them to wear as necklaces.

Thomas Jefferson, author of the Declaration of Independence, became the third U.S. president in 1801. During his term, the shape of the Indian Peace medals evolved from oval to round as the design was simplified. There remained three sizes; a large example can be found on page 122. One side features Jefferson's profile with the inscription, "Th. Jefferson President of the U.S. A.D. 1801." On the reverse, "Peace and Friendship" are inscribed, while a crossed peace pipe and tomahawk, as well as clasped hands, adorn the piece's center. The left hand features the cuff of a military uniform, with three braided chevrons; the right is that of a Native American, wearing a silver cuff with an engraved American eagle, as he pledges allegiance to the U.S.

The design of the Jefferson Peace medal was the basis for the 2004 nickel celebrating the 200TH anniversary of the Louisiana Purchase.

This acquisition of 828,800 square miles of Louisiana from Napoléon I, consisting today of fourteen states and two Canadian provinces, cost nearly $15 million. Soon after the purchase, President Jefferson commissioned Meriwether Lewis and William Clark to explore the new territory. Many Jefferson Peace medals were distributed to the Indians during this expedition as part of an effort to assure Natives that the expedition party sought peace. According to a proposed but never enacted regulation by Lewis and Clark, whose overland expedition was the first to reach the Pacific and back, exploring the territories acquired by the Louisiana Purchase, "large medals will be given to principal village chiefs, medium will be given to the principal war chiefs, and the smallest given to less distinguished chiefs and warriors." These unofficial regulations dictated that, "whenever a foreign medal is worn, it will be replaced by an American medal assuming the Indian is entitled to a medal."

Robert Wilson Hoge

Robert Wilson Hoge, Curator of North American Coins and Currency, American Numismatic Society since 2001. Mr. Hoge's numismatic interests range widely through ancient, medieval, oriental and early modern issues. He has participated in a number of archaeological projects, and in 1985 was invited to observe the treasure salvage of the 1622 Spanish galleon *Nuestra Señora de Atocha*. He has been a member of numerous professional numismatic and museological organizations and has served as a speaker upon many occasions, and has appeared on the PBS Television programs, *The News Hour with Jim Lehrer* and *The History Detectives*.

How did the peace medal evolve from a European to an American tradition? How did the American tradition change over time?

Large coins and medals displaying rulers' effigies became a hallmark of prestige among European potentates in the Renaissance. Medallic portraits found their way into international diplomacy as gifts. From an early period, European colonial powers sought to win and hold the loyalty and support, if not the love and admiration, of Native American peoples by making gifts of the same kinds of items. Thus, as a demonstration of sovereignty, certain medals came to play an important role in the development of the Americas. They tangibly linked leading natives with their foreign overlords. A 1632 silver medal of Cecil Calvert and Anne Arundel, Lord and Lady Baltimore, may have been such a one in the Early British Colonial period. In Virginia, a decree of 1661 called for engraved plates to be given to local Indians as badges.

By the early eighteenth century, presentation of royal medals to Indians had become well-established in the New World as Britain, France, and Spain contended to obtain dominance. A standard "Indian medal" was first minted by the British under George I, with three obverse and six reverse types. The British North American colonies produced their own first efforts as a part of this international rivalry in the 1750s. Great Britain gained hegemony and rewarded loyal tribal leaders with large silver medals bearing a portrait of King George III. With the revolt of his Atlantic seaboard colonies in the 1770s, the king's government had a new need to present medals to natives to reward their support in military ventures against the American rebels, a practice which endured through the period of the War of 1812.

The government of the United States, in the 1780s and 90s and early 1800s, countered the British and, in the south, Spanish diplomacy by a distribution of its own medals intended to promote peace and friendship toward the new country. Traditionally, such medals were relatively substantial pieces, struck in silver; no doubt to impress the natives, the Americans produced the largest yet. But due to the United States' lack of minting capacity, President Washington's administration had to content itself by commissioning appropriately hand-engraved oval silver plates from silversmiths and ultimately, and ignominiously, ordering a series of presentation medals from the British manufacturing firm of Boulton and Watt. From Thomas Jefferson's administration through the end of the Indian

Wars in the 1880s, the United States regularly issued a special series of medals designed to promote effective good will between the "Great White Father" in Washington and his Indian "children." The designs chosen, apart from the portraits of the successive presidents, changed from dignified, traditional, symbolic depictions of clasped hands and peace pipes to representational images of the advantages of the "settled" European-type lifestyle. Some even contrasted this with the gruesome savagery of scalping, in an unfavorable allusion to supposedly native practices.

Originally, Indian Peace medals were among the most important diplomatic gifts of State. By the later nineteenth century, however, they had come to be regarded by the government as rather trifling rewards for good conduct—although this was perhaps not fully perceived by the recipients, who often cherished them greatly.

The current debate about immigration was vividly portrayed in medals produced in the first half of the nineteenth century. Tell us about that heated debate with respect to the Columbian Order (Tammany) AR Badge and the Society of the American Volunteers AR Badge.

There are indeed certain American medals of the nineteenth century that relate in interesting ways to the constant American themes of immigration and the integration of different groups into the

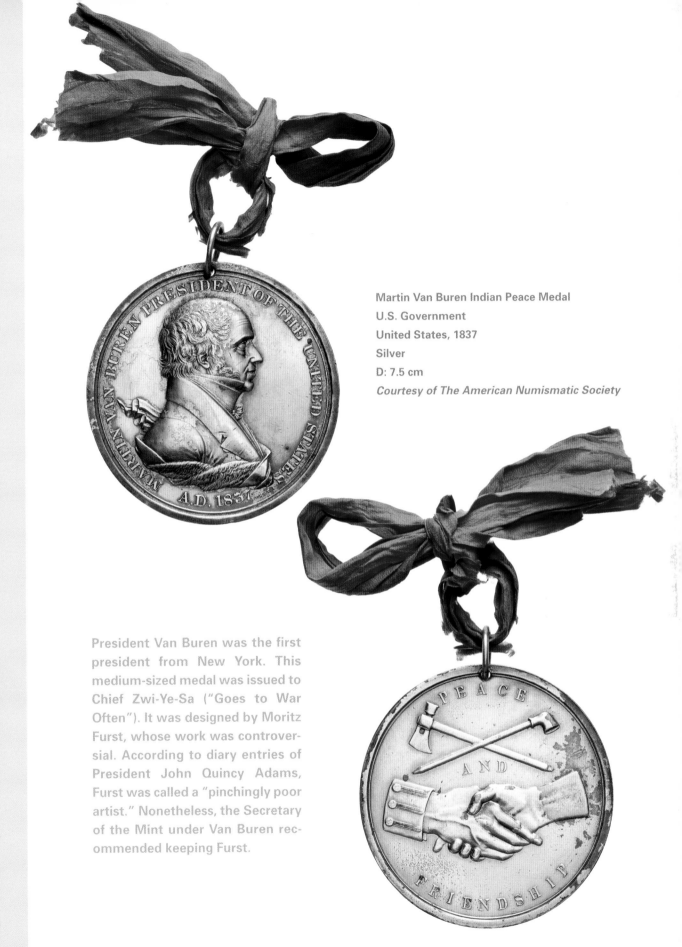

Martin Van Buren Indian Peace Medal
U.S. Government
United States, 1837
Silver
D: 7.5 cm
Courtesy of The American Numismatic Society

President Van Buren was the first president from New York. This medium-sized medal was issued to Chief Zwi-Ye-Sa ("Goes to War Often"). It was designed by Moritz Furst, whose work was controversial. According to diary entries of President John Quincy Adams, Furst was called a "pinchingly poor artist." Nonetheless, the Secretary of the Mint under Van Buren recommended keeping Furst.

The Indian peace medals changed dramatically during President Fillmore's administration. The silver medals were made in New York rather than the U.S. Mint in Philadelphia with new engravings. The words "PEACE" and "FRIENDSHIP" were removed and there were no longer three sizes of medals, but only two. This medal, which was issued to Deaf Bull, Crow, is an example of a larger medal.

Millard Fillmore Indian Peace Medal
U.S. Government
United States, 1850
Silver
D: 7.52 cm
Courtesy of The American Numismatic Society

Andrew Johnson Indian Peace Medal
U.S. Mint
United States, 1865
Silver
D: 7.52 cm
Courtesy of The American Numismatic Society

The President Johnson peace medal is radically different from those preceding. The engraver was Anthony Paquet from Pennsylvania. The design on the back portrays the bust of George Washington on a pedestal with the word "PEACE" inside a laurel wreath. Machinery covers the foreground and there is a railroad in the background.

Ulysses S. Grant Indian Peace Medal
U.S. Mint
United States, 1871
Silver
D: 6.3 cm
*Courtesy of The American
Numismatic Society*

fabric of society in the United States. And both sides make their appeal in the form of patriotism. As an example, a rare badge of the Columbian Order (pages 14 and 15) was a medallic emblem worn by members of a group that came to be famous for espousing the cause of newly arrived citizens. This was in fact the official name of the New York branch of the Society of St. Tammany—better known in later years as Tammany Hall, after the location of its meeting place. By nurturing and marshalling immigrants, the Tammany brethren were eventually able to weld their constituency into a powerful

political force, notoriously corrupt yet beneficial in many ways for generations of newcomers.

Tammany was basically a fraternal society. There were many of these, of various kinds, in the early years of the American Republic, ranging from religious zealot and college student groups to anti-slavery movements, to leisure clubs, to social charities, self-help groups and feminist and temperance societies, to intellectual roundtables and experimental communes and to quasi-military formations. Some were relatively open and well-known—like the national political parties; others,

such as the Underground Railroad and Vigilante Committees, depended upon complete secrecy.

Like the original Society of the Cincinnati, the brotherhood of officers who had served in the Continental Army with General Washington during the Revolutionary War, the Tammany Society was a patriotic body dedicated to the well-being of the young country. But it was much more of a populist group, whereas the Society of the Cincinnati was regarded as tending to be more elitist. The "Tammanies" adopted pseudo-American Indian terms, offices and practices, calling their headquarters "wigwams" and

This is an extremely rare peace medal issued to Bear-Who-Lies-Down, Yanktonai. During President Garfield's administration the medals were made in bronze, not in silver, unlike this example. The medals were no longer round and the design and production were under the office of the U.S. Mint rather than the Indian office.

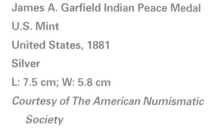

James A. Garfield Indian Peace Medal
U.S. Mint
United States, 1881
Silver
L: 7.5 cm; W: 5.8 cm
Courtesy of The American Numismatic Society

their elected leaders "sachems" or "sagamores," for instance. They developed out of anti-British patriot enclaves in each of the original thirteen states, and tended to have an urban focus. While their political motives and operations may often have been hidden, their presence and focus were not.

A completely different outlook was held by a group called the American Volunteers—actually a "wing" of the secretive mid-nineteenth century anti-immigrant political party known as the Know-Nothings, who issued a rare badge in 1856 (page 64) to recognize excellence in militia drill. The group wanted to alienate foreigners, and some members were evidently prepared to fight off newcomers at the borders. The Know-Nothing Volunteers imploded shortly afterward, when they could not decide as a group whether they were pro- or anti-slavery. Today, it is difficult to discover much about this elusive group, or the nature of the militia activities for which it made the award.

During the Civil War medals were forged from coins. What is the origin of this trend? Did it continue?

There had been an old tradition of using coins as the basis for medals. The first American versions of European Indian Peace medals, in fact, had been minted out of Spanish colonial "pieces-of-eight"—standard eight-reales coins. Later, school and societal award medals had sometimes been created by polishing smooth and then hand-engraving their surfaces of coins. This was not a common practice, however, and was resorted to by those who, for whatever reason, might need to take a short cut. The Southern Confederacy, for instance, found itself technologically lacking during most of the Civil War. This is the reason why the most celebrated medal issue of the Confederate States of America, or rather of the great state of Texas under the Confederacy's auspices, was made out of old Mexican coins!

The Battle of the Sabine pass was an astonishing victory for the Texans. In a fluke of history, one company—the Davis Guards, consisting largely of Galveston "wharfies"—stopped the entire Union invasion. Each of the several dozen heroes, under the command of Lieutenant Richard "Dick" Dowling, was given an engraved medal, seen on page 67, in commemoration of their spectacular day and deed. This was a private endeavor, and whereas there were silver workers in Texas, there was no minting facility. Each medal was a planed-down Mexican peso (piece of eight) with a simple bent bar attached at the top as a loop for a fastening, hand-engraved with the necessary details of the engagement at the mouth of the Sabine River.

The practice of using older coins as hosts for later medals, badges, emblems, or jewelry items (of-ten in the form of "love tokens") has continued through to modern times, unbeknownst to most people.

Badges represent particular actions or encounters. What is the significance of the Civil War Corps badges?

Some of the badges or medals worn by soldiers in the Civil War did relate to encounters their units had witnessed, but most were emblems intended for recognition and to encourage an *esprit-de-corps* in the respective formations. What makes them fascinating is the fact that as markers of the particular units, we can follow them through the histories of the campaigns in which the owners played a part. Some of them had the original owner's name engraved onto them. The use of medals or decorations as awards to denote bravery, service, or heroism was a very new custom in the United States at this time. Certain officers simply had badges made as gifts to distribute to their men.

The Medal of Honor has a long and glorious history dating from the Civil War. What is the difference, if any, from those first issued and today?

The Medal of Honor, the highest award for bravery presented by the United States military, has changed somewhat in appearance during the course of its history, depending upon just when they were actually issued. They have always been made as star-shaped pendants, with space on the back for adding a dedicatory inscription, but early versions were made of bronze, while from 1904, they were gilded, with a wreath added.

The attachment ribbons and manner of wearing the medals have changed several times. The first had a short ribbon that featured elements of the American flag suspended from a pin. The version for the Navy used a small anchor as the ribbon's fixture for loops at the top of the medal, while the Army version used a small spread-eagle emblem. In 1896, so that it could stand out more distinctively, the ribbon was changed to a simple red, white, and blue line design because, in the post-Civil War era, many other unofficial decorations had usurped the appearance of the highly esteemed Medal of Honor.

The form of the medal and ribbon still used today is that of 1904, when a light blue silk ribbon sprinkled with white stars was adopted. It then became customary for the medal to be worn around the recipient's neck, although small versions have been authorized as emblematic pins as well. Each branch of the military services today has its own slightly variant form of the Medal of Honor. Altogether, more than 3,400 of the medals have been awarded since the establishment of the honor in 1861 or 1862. Many of the medals have been awarded posthumously, and consequently never worn at all.

Cannot Be Thrown Down, a Warrior
George Catlin
Kansas, 1832
Smithsonian American Art Museum,
*   Washington, D.C.*

Ensuring peace and capturing the natives' loyalty was most important to the Head of the Indian Office, later to become the Bureau of Indian Affairs. Renowned American artist, George Catlin, accompanied several of Clark's missions into Native American territory, immortalizing his subjects in paintings and prints showing the natives wearing their important Peace Medals. Medals were often the focal point of the work as evidenced in the remarkable painting of *Jee-hé-o-hóShah, Cannot Be Thrown Down, a Warrior,* seen on page 130.

The Abraham Lincoln Peace medal on page 131 is unique because of its history. According to the American Numismatic Society, the medal was sold in 1873 by a Ute Indian chief. In a fight with another tribe, his assailant fired a bullet which embedded in the medal and saved the chief's life. The chief, however, believed the Peace medal possessed supernatural powers and should have completely deflected the bullet. As a result, the chief disposed of the medal as "bad medicine." The bullet is still embedded in the medal, cutting

into the engraved images, which had again been reformed during the administration of James Buchanan, Lincoln's predecessor. The natives are in the outer circle with one scalping another, accompanied by a quiver of arrows, a bow, peace pipe, and the head of an Indian woman. At the center of the medal is a native plowing a field, with Americans playing baseball in front of a church and house. During the Civil War, baseball became extremely popular, resulting in the creation of the National Association of Baseball Players, yet it is rare to see the "national pastime" engraved on an official medal. The Commissioner of Indian Affairs asked if the Indian headdress on the man plowing could be removed, but since the die had already been cut, the feathers stayed.

The last Indian Peace medals bore the portrait of President Benjamin Harrison, as seen on page 131. The urging for this medal came from the Native Americans themselves, namely the Otoe and Missouri tribes who, in early 1890, offered to pay for silver Peace medals. The engraver, Charles E. Barber, designed two circles on the medal's reverse: the one on the left reads "Paul T. Boynton, Arapahoe Tribe" showing a Native American Indian in front of his tepee. The right circle, featuring what we can assume to be a Native American in farmer's clothes, holding a horse and shovel, reads "Cheyenne & Arapahoe Agency, OT, Nov. 18, 1890." The word "Peace" with the now-familiar peace pipe and tomahawk were engraved near the top, while "Progress" and the image of a plow can be seen at the bottom. According to Prucha, "the largest numbers of Harrison medals were presented to Cheyenne and Arapahoe Chiefs who cooperated with the U.S. government in opening their land. . . . Each Indian was to receive an allotment of 160 acres while the rest of the reservation was sold to the U.S. government for $1.5 million."

At the end of the Great War some 28 years later, during the negotiations of the Treaty of Versailles, U.S. President Woodrow Wilson lobbied successfully for the creation of a League of Nations, which would arbitrate disputes and

Abraham Lincoln Indian Peace Medal
U.S. Mint
United States, 1862
Silver
D: 7.4–7.7 cm
Courtesy of The American Numismatic Society

Benjamin Harrison Indian Peace Medal
U.S. Mint
United States, 1890
Silver
D: 7.6 cm
Courtesy of The American Numismatic Society

Arc de Triomphe Brooch
Cartier
Paris, 1919
Gold, platinum, diamonds, sapphire, rubies,
   emeralds, topazes, onyx
L: 4.6 cm; W: 3.9 cm
Cartier Collection

hopefully avoid future conflicts as bloody as The War to End All Wars. However, Wilson could not persuade his Congress that America should join the League, leading to Supreme Allied Army Commander Maréchal Ferdinand Foch's cynical and prescient declaration: "This is not peace. It is an armistice for 20 years."

There is little jewelry commemorating the peace following WWI, but two such master-pieces came from Cartier Paris. One, entitled Arc de Triomphe Brooch, page 132, was created with gold, platinum, diamonds, sapphire cabachons, rubies, emeralds, topazes, and onyx. The sapphire cabachons represent the helmets of the soldiers who marched down the Champs-Elysées to celebrate victory in WWI, on Bastille Day, July 14, 1919. On top of the Arc de Triomphe on this brooch, and on the one on page 133, are the flags representing the allied victors of the Great War. The second Cartier brooch captures the same theme but was created as a flag with the Arc de Triomphe in the center. This extraordinary brooch consists of platinum, gold, diamonds, rubies, sapphires, jacinth, emeralds, and onyx. It was sold to Sir Bhupindra Singh, one of Cartier's largest clients. At that time, Singh was the ruling Maharaja of Patiala (Punjab region of India) and an Honorary Lieutenant Colonel in 1918.

During WWII, both French and American jewelers produced many precious objects celebrating the causes of liberation and peace. At first, French jewelers created jeweled birds in cages to signify France being occupied. In August 1944, when France was liberated, the jeweled birds were free, so the cage doors were able to open.

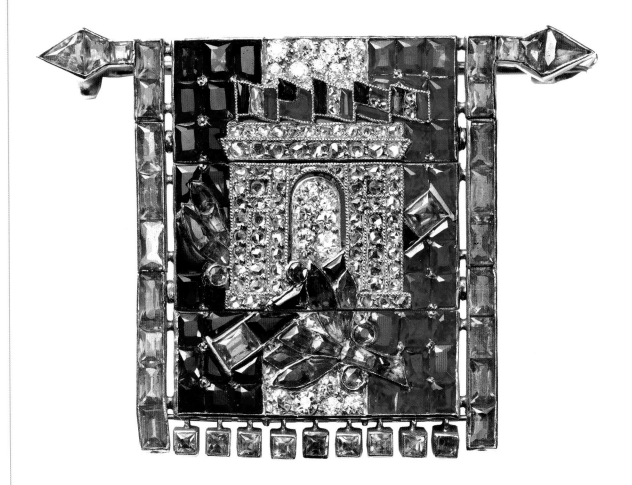

Arc de Triomphe Flag Brooch
Cartier
Paris, 1919
Gold, platinum, diamonds, rubies, sapphires, emeralds, onyx
W: 2.94 cm; H: 4.1 cm
Cartier Collection

American jewelers celebrated their country's role in freeing Europe by fashioning the large two-inch Liberation Jeep Brooch on page 134, made of 14-karat gold and rubies with movable wheels. This pin is a stylized version of a World War II Willys MB Jeep manufactured between 1941 and 1945. During WWII, jeeps were the main car of the U.S. Army and its allies, and more than 600,000 jeeps were produced. Still well-liked today, there is a 1952 jeep in the collection of New York's Museum of Modern Art's Department of Architecture and Design.

The American jeweler Tiffany celebrated the victory in Europe by creating V-shaped brooches. The brooch on page 134 was made in gold and enamel and dated from 1941 to 1945. On page 135 is a Tiffany jeweled diamond, ruby, and sapphire ring, also in the V-shaped design.

Another V charm, created by Cartier in 1943, on page 135, is elaborately fashioned out

Victory Ring
Tiffany & Co.
United States, c. 1941–1945
Gold, diamonds, rubies, sapphires
H: 1.3 cm; W: 1.7 cm
Tiffany & Co. Archives

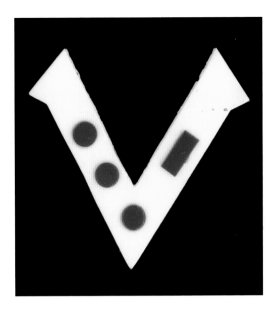

"V for Victory" Badge
Maker unknown
United Kingdom, 1940–1945
Plastic, metal
D: .6 cm; W: 4.5 cm; H: 4.3 cm
Imperial War Museum (EPH 528)

Union Jack Pin
Maker unknown
England, c. 1890
15k gold, enamel
L: 3.8 cm
Courtesy of A La Vieille Russie

V Charm
Cartier
Paris, 1943
Platinum, diamonds,
    rubies, sapphire
L: 1.5 cm; W: 1.37 cm
Cartier Collection

135

Star of the Grand Cross of the Iron Cross
Maker unknown
Germany, 1939
Silver, black enamel
Star: L: 8.6 cm
West Point Museum Collection, United States
Military Academy, West Point, New York

of diamonds, rubies, and sapphires, symbolizing colors of the French flag. It is amusing that the diamonds across the baguette V correspond to the letter V in the Morse Code. Much like the "V" pins worn to show patriotism fifty years earlier in 1890, the British Flag Pin on page 135 was worn after the defeat of the Boer States (the Orange Free State and the Transval Republic) to express Britain's pride in their formidable Empire.

Not all symbolic aspirations of liberation were realized. On page 136 is Prussia and Germany's highest military decoration, the Star of the Grand Cross of the Iron Cross, first worn under the rule of King Frederick William III of Prussia as his government appealed to the citizens of Prussia to aid in his war against Napoléon by contributing gold to buy armaments. As a result, in Berlin, iron jewelry became fashionable as an expression of patriotism. Karl Fredrich Schinkel designed the iron cross to recall the fourteenth century Teutonic Knights. The Star of the Grand Cross of the Iron Cross

was only given out at the end of a battle to the most successful general: in 1815, after Napoléon's defeat at Waterloo, Prussian Field Marshal Gebhart Leberecht von Blücher was awarded the Cross; Paul von Hindenburg, Chief of the General Staff was awarded the medal in 1918 for his 1914 decisive victory on the Eastern front in the Battle of Tannenberg killing nearly 80,000 Russians and an additional 90,000 Russian prisoners of war. He was also awarded the Cross. The Star of the Grand Cross on page 136 that was created but never presented. It is now part of the West Point Museum's collection. This star

was seized from a German bunker in 1945 by the U.S. Army. The star was originally commissioned by Deputy Fuhrer Hermann Göring, who intended to present it to Hitler when the Nazis defeated the British and captured the British Isles. This, of course, never happened, so the star was never presented.

Also commemorating peace and liberation, on page 137, is a beautiful 18-karat gold Cartier cigarette case with sapphires, signed by General de Gaulle, given to Allied Commander Dwight D. Eisenhower whose wartime rank of 5-star general (his Circle of Stars is pictured on page

Cigarette Case—Gift from Général Charles de Gaulle
Cartier
Paris, 1945
Gold, platinum, sapphires
L: 11.7 cm; W: 8.1 cm
Dwight D. Eisenhower Presidential Library and Museum

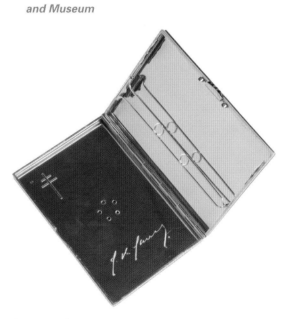

Cigarette Case (interior)

Cigarette Case
Cartier
Paris, 1945
Gold
W: 13 cm; D: 8 cm; H: 1.05 cm
Cartier Collection

Liseuse Paper Knife
Cartier
Paris, 1945
Silver
H: 12 cm; W: 1.84 cm
Cartier Collection

69) corresponded to that of European Field Marshal. General de Gaulle gave this Cartier cigarette case to Eisenhower on the occasion of his visit to Paris on June 14, 1945, just after VE (Victory in Europe) Day on May 8, 1945. De Gaulle, owing to his imperious attitude but minor share of arms and men, had a strained relationship with all of the allied leaders. However, as Eisenhower and de Gaulle were military

men and thought alike, they had a mutually respectful relationship. The inside lid is etched with the Cross of Lorraine, originally the symbol of Joan of Arc, which meant a great deal to de Gaulle, the leader of Free France whose name Eisenhower had helped make a reality. Since Lorraine (the region borders with Belgium, Luxembourg, and Germany) was annexed to Germany between 1871 and 1918 and again in

1940 through 1944, de Gaulle chose it as the symbol of French resistance for his Gaullist movement. The French President displayed the Cross on cigarette cases and knives like those on pages 138 and 139. There is a silver Cartier paper cutter with a Cross of Lorraine image. The 18-karat gold cigarette case not only has de Gaulle's signature, but also its origin with the inscription "BRUXELLES 10 ET 11 OCTOBRE 1945."

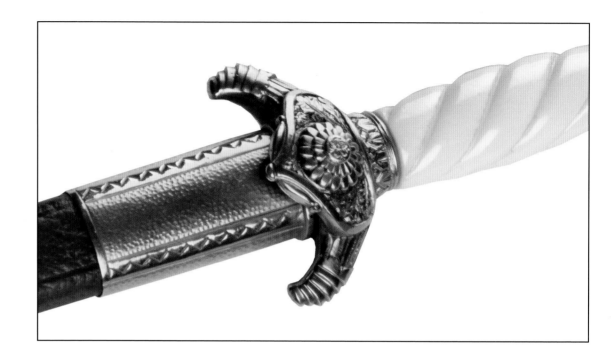

As Eisenhower and the allies invaded from the west, Soviet Marshal Georgy Zhukov and his armies advanced from the east. On page 140 is a beautiful ivory, bone, and gold dagger with a Russian inscription on the blade. This dagger was given to General Eisenhower by Marshal Zhukov on the occasion of the visit of the Marshal, Deputy Commissioner for Foreign Affairs, Andrey Vyshinsky, and 20 officers of the Red Army to Allied Headquarters in Frankfurt Germany for a victory celebration in early June 1945. It was during this visit that Mashal Zhukov decorated General Eisenhower and Field Marshal Montgomery with the Order of Victory on June 10, 1945. The Soviet Order of Victory was designed by Joseph Stalin and consists of a diamond oval with a star in the center with red stones.

Dagger—Gift from Marshal Grigori K. Zhukov
Maker unknown
Union of Soviet Socialist Republic, 1945
Ivory, metal
L: 28.6 cm; W: 5.1 cm
*Dwight D. Eisenhower Presidential Library
   and Museum*

This commemorative bell was made from a German aircraft shot down over Britain. It features the heads of Roosevelt, Churchill, and Stalin. The handle shows a "V" for victory. Bells such as this one were sold to aid the RAF (Royal Air Force) Benevolent Fund.

Victory Bell
Conrad A. Parlanti
London, 1945
Metal (alloy) from shot-down German aircraft
H: 16.2 cm; D: 11.5 cm
Imperial War Museum (EPH 6975)

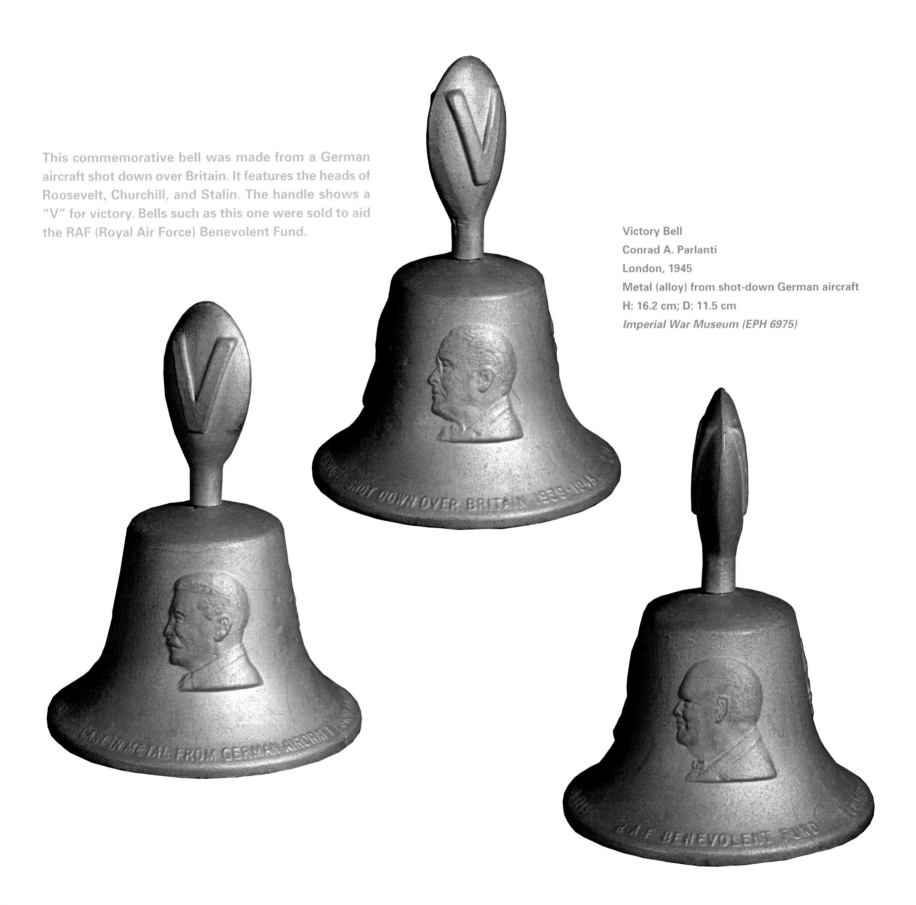

ACKNOWLEDGMENTS

Many prominent experts of leading institutions in the United States, Britain, and France aided my writing of this book. They include: the American Numismatic Society Executive Director Ute Wartenberg Kagan, Curator of North American Coins and Currency Robert Wilson Hoge, and Collections Manager Dr. Elena Stolyarik; the British Museum Keeper of Coins and Medals Philip Attwood; the Imperial War Museum, London, Director General Diane Lees and Head of the Department of Collections Access Fergus Read; the Musée de l'Armée Directeur Christian Baptiste, Directeur Adjoint David Guillet, Conservateur Départment des Deux Guerres Mondiales Lieutenant-Colonel Christophe Bertrand, Conservateur du Patrimoine Départment Moderne Emilie Robbe, Conservateur Adjoint Emmanuel Ranvoisy, and Responsable du Fond Emblematique et Décoration Lucie Villeneuve de Janti; the National Army Museum, London,

Assistant Director (Collections) Dr. Peter B. Boyden and Head of Exhibits Gillian Brewer; the Natural History Museum of Los Angeles County Collections Manager Beth Werling; Richard Edgcumbe and Clare Phillips of the Department of Sculpture, Metalwork, Ceramics and Glass at the Victoria and Albert Museum, London; and the West Point Museum Director David M. Reel and Curator of History Michael J. McAfee.

The patrimony of leading firms have also contributed to this exhibition. They include: A La Vieille Russie and its Directors Peter L. Schaffer and Mark A. Schaffer; Alfred Dunhill and its Archivist Curator Zia Fernandez; Boucheron and its President Jean-Christophe Bedos; Maison Cartier and its President Bernard Fornas, its Image, Style and Heritage Director and good friend Pierre Rainero, and its Curator of the Cartier Collection Pascale Lepeu; Chaumet and its President Thierry Fritsch, its Curator of the

Chaumet Museum and Archives Beatrice de Plinval, and its Cultural Heritage Deputy Mélanie Sallois; Hermès International and its CEO Patrick Thomas, Jérôme Guerrand-Hermès, Président du Conseil de Surveillance d'Hermès International, and its Directrice du Patrimoine Culturel Menehould du Chatelle de Bazelaire; Daniel Morris and Denis Gallion of Historical Design; Tom Heyman of Oscar Heyman, Inc.; and Tiffany & Co. and its CEO and Chairman Michael J. Kowalski and its Archivist Annamarie V. Sandecki.

Other important experts, contributors, and lenders to *Lest We Forget: Masterpieces of Patriotic Jewelry and Military Decorations* include Yvonne Markowitz, Museum of Fine Arts, Boston, Rita J. and Susan B. Kaplan Curator of Jewelry; Collectors Bruno Ledoux, Stuart Rabin, and Jean-Pascal Tranié; and the President of Fondation Josée et René de Chambrun Georges Renand. Other colleagues who encouraged me throughout this undertaking with their knowledge include: Hervé Aaron, President of Didier Aaron; Henri de Castries, CEO of AXA Art Insurance Corporation; Renaud Dutreil, Chairman of LVMH USA; Sotheby's experts, Vice Chairman David Redden and Aaron Rich; Anne Eisenhower, granddaughter of President Dwight D. Eisenhower; and George Patton Waters, grandson of General Patton, who inspired me to a new challenge. I would also like to thank Consul General of France in New York Philippe Lalliot.

Other important supporters include National Jewelry Institute Board Member Christiane Fischer, President & CEO of AXA Art Insurance Corporation, who has supported the National Jewelry Institute's past seventeen exhibitions; and Global CEO of AXA Art Insurance Dr. Ulrich Guntram. I also want to thank the following: American Folk Art Museum, New York, Senior Curator Stacy C. Hollander; the British Museum's Benjamin Alsop, Janet Larkin, Keith Lowe, and Kristen Wenger; the Dwight D. Eisenhower Presidential Library and Museum; La Fondation Josée et René de Chambrun's I. Sophie Grivet; Hermès International's Malvina Girard, Guigone Rolland, and Marc Stoltz; Historical Design's Manuela Zissler-Grenert; Imperial War Museum's Louise Macfarlane; the Ledoux Napoléon Collection Curator, Georgina Letourmy; the National Army Museum's Curator of Fine and Decorative Art Robert Fleming and Ian Jones; the Patton Museum of Cavalry and Armor Director Arthur L. Dyer and Curator Charles Lemons; James McConnaughy of Shrubsole; the Victoria and Albert Museum, London's Peter Ellis, David Packer, Roxanne Peters, and Rebecca Wallace; the West Point Museum's Marlana L. Cook; as well as John Ortved; Christine Fourneau; Richard Michalski; Lucia Suljic; and Allison Barker.

I want to thank my husband, Peter, who taught me discipline. Peter was a First Lieutenant in the Air Force. He grew up in Fort Huachuca, Arizona, where his father trained before serving as a Captain in the South Pacific during World War II.

I finally must thank our very dedicated Board of Trustees who have encouraged and guided the development of the National Jewelry Institute: Ashton Hawkins, Chairman; Hervé Aaron; Christiane Fischer; Christopher Forbes; Chantal Miller; and Peter O. Price.

PHOTO CREDITS

Page 116: Oscar Heyman

Page 130: Smithsonian American Art Museum, Washington, D.C. / Art Resource, New York

Page 139: Nils Herrmann, Cartier Collection © Cartier

BIBLIOGRAPHY

A Sacred Relic: The Washington-Lafayette Cincinnati Medal. New York: Sotheby's, Inc., 2007.

Attwood, Philip. *Badges.* London: British Museum Press, 2004.

Basily-Callimaki, Mme E. de. *J.B. Isabey; Sa vie, Son temps, 1767–1855, Suivi du Catalogue de L'Oeuvre Gravée par et d'Apres Isabey.* Paris: Frazier-Soye, 1909.

Birch, Diana, Richard Bishop and John Haywood. *British Battles and Medals,* Seventh Edition. London: Spink & Son Ltd., 2006.

Chaumet, Joaillier Depuis 1780. Paris, 1995.

Chaille, François and Eric Nussbaum. *The Cartier Collection.* Paris: Flammarion, 2004.

Clifford, Anne. *Cut-Steel and Berlin Iron Jewellery.* Bath: Adams & Dart, 1971.

Collins, Larry and Dominique Lapierre. *Is Paris Burning?* New York: Castle Books, 2000.

D'Este, Carlo. *Eisenhower: A Soldier's Life.* New York: Henry Holt and Company, LLC, 2002.

D'Este, Carlo. *Patton: A Genius for War.* New York: Harper Collins, 1995.

Dion-Tenenbaum, Anne. *L'Orfevre de Napoléon; Martin-Guillaume Biennais.* Paris: Reunion des Musees Nationaux, 2003.

Dorling, H. Taprell. *Ribbons and Medals.* London: Osprey Publishing Ltd, 1983.

Duckers, Peter. *European Orders and Decorations to 1945.* Oxford: Shire Publications, 2008.

Dymond, Steve. *Researching British Military Medals—A Practical Guide.* Wiltshire: Crowood Press Ltd., 2007.

Ferling, John. *The Ascent of George Washington: The Hidden Political Genius of an American Icon.* New York: Bloomsbury Press, 2009.

Fondation Napoléon. *Trésors de la Fondation Napoléon. Dans l'Intimité de la Cour Impériale.* Paris: Musée Jacquemart-André Nouveau Monde Editions, 2004.

Glass, Charles. *Americans in Paris: Life and Death under Nazi Occupation, 1940–1944.* London: Harper Press, 2009.

Grice, Elizabeth. "I Wouldn't Have Been as Brave." *The Daily Telegraph* 08 Nov. 2006: 25

Humair, Sylviane. "Les Morel fabricants de tabatières de recompense." *Gazette de l'Hôtel Drouot* 12, 21 (1986): 40-42.

Jacobs, Martin S. *V for Victory Collectibles.* Missoula: Pictorial Histories Pub., 2001.

Jean-Baptiste Isabey portraitiste de l'Europe. Musées et domaine nationaux de Compiègne. Paris: Réunion des Musées Nationaux, 2005.

Joslin, Edward C. *The Observer's Book of British Awards and Medals.* London: Frederick Warne & Co Ltd, 1975.

Kilroe, Edwin Patrick. *Saint Tammany and the Origin of the Society of Tammany or Columbian Order in the City of New York.* New York: Edwin Patrick Kilroe, 1913.

Kimball, Jane A. *Trench Art: An Illustrated History.* Davis: Silverpenny Press, 2004.

Kuehne, Richard E. and Michael J. McAfee. *The West Point Museum: A Guide to the Collections.* West Point: Association of Graduates, the Class of 1932, United States Military Academy, 1987.

Lemoine-Bouchard, Nathalie, *Les Peintures en Miniature: 1650–1850*. Les editions de l'Amateur, 2008.

Lundin, Steve. "G.I. Joe Tells Time." *International Watch*. 2009. *iW Magazine* 10 Nov. 2009 <http://www.iwmagazine.com/current_issue_detail.cfm/ArticleID/544.>

Mackay, James, John W. Mussell and Philip Mussell. *The Medal Yearbook 2008*. Devon: Token Publishing Ltd., 2007.

Markowitz, Yvonne and Midori Ferris. "Charm Bracelets, Portable Autobiographies." *Ornament Magazine*. Summer 1998: 54-57.

Maze-Sencier, Alphonse. *Les Fournisseurs de Napoléon Ier et des deux Impératrices*. Paris: Henri Laurens, 1893.

Maze-Sencier, Alphonse. *Le Livre des Collectionneurs*. Paris: Librarie Renouard, 1885.

Miller, Merle. *Ike the Soldier: As They Knew Him*. New York: G.P. Putnam's Sons, 1987.

Narbeth, Colin. *Collecting Military Medals: A Beginner's Guide*. Cambridge: The Lutterworth Press, 2002.

Patton, Robert H. *The Pattons: A Personal History of an American Family*. New York: Crown Publishers, 1994.

Perry. Mark. *Partners in Command: George Marshall and Dwight Eisenhower in War and Peace*. New York: The Penguin Press, 2007

Phillips, Clare. *Bejewelled by Tiffany, 1837–1987*. London: Yale University Press, 2006.

Phillips, Clare. *Jewels & Jewellery*. London: V&A Publishing, 2008.

Prins, Harold E.L. "Two George Washington Medals: Missing Links in the Chain of Friendship between the United States and the Wabanaki Confederacy."
  The Medal, 7 (Winter 1985): 9-11.

Prucha, Francis Paul. *Indian Peace Medals in American History*. Bluffton: Rivilo Books, 1994.

Purves, Alec A. *Collecting Medals and Decorations*. London: Seaby, 1978.

Rendell, Kenneth W. *World War II: Saving the Reality: A Collector's Vault*. Atlanta: Whitman Publishing, 2009

Roberts, Andrew. *Masters and Commanders: How Four Titans Won the War in the West, 1941–1945*. New York: Harper Collins, 2009.

Schmuttermeier, Elisabeth. *Cast Iron from Central Europe, 1800–1850*. New York: Bard Graduate Center for Studies in the Decorative Arts, 1995.

Snider, Nicholas D. *Antique Sweetheart Jewelry*. Atglen: Schiffer Publishing, 1996.

Snider, Nicholas D. *Sweetheart Jewelry and Collectibles*. Atglen: Schiffer Publishing, 1995.

Spencer, William. *Medals: The Researcher's Guide*. Surrey: The National Archives, 2006.

Spotts, Frederic. *The Shameful Peace: How French Artists and Intellectuals Survived the Nazi Occupation*. New Haven: Yale University Press, 2008.

Strouse, Jean. "J. Pierpont Morgan: Financier and Collector." *The Metropolitan Museum of Art Bulletin* 57, 3 (2000): 1, 3-64.

The F.D.R. Cartier Victory Clock. New York: Sotheby's, Inc., 2007.

"The Pilgrimage to Metz." *The Columbiad* XXVII, 8.

Tulard, Jean. *Dictionnaire Napoléon*. Paris: Editions Fayard, 1987.

Washington, George. *Confederate Series The Papers of George Washington*. Charlottesville: University 3Press of Virginia, 1992.

Weeks, John W. "America's Welcome to Foch." *Columbia* November 1921: 1, 13.

INDEX